KU-105-105

contents

contents

Grammar

Collins Easy Learning English Conversation: Book 2 is a completely new type of book for learners of English of all ages. It will help you to increase your confidence in holding a conversation in English in a variety of situations.

To sound natural in a foreign language, you need to know both the words and the grammar. However, it can be difficult to put these two things together and be sure that what you are saying sounds like natural English. *Easy Learning English Conversation* has been carefully designed to give you whole sentences which you can use with confidence in all your conversations.

Collins Easy Learning English Conversation is made up of 14 units, each giving the language used in a particular situation, for instance shopping, travelling or talking about your health.

In each unit, the language is arranged by language task, for example, 'saying what you want' or 'making suggestions'. Clear headings help you to find what you need. 'Good to know' boxes give advice about important or tricky points.

You will find examples of all the phrases covered, and the words in them are explained at the bottom of each page.

At the end of each unit is a page called 'Listen out for', which gives more useful phrases that you may hear or need to use in each situation. This is followed by a conversation, showing the phrases you have learned in a natural situation. You can listen to these conversations on the CD that comes with this book. The CD also contains some useful phrases you can listen to and then practise saying.

After the 14 units, the 'all the phrases by function...' chapter arranges the phrases by language task. So, for example, all the phrases for 'complaining' come together.

Finally, there is a grammar section, giving useful advice on important grammar points, such as how to form tenses, and the differences between countable and uncountable nouns.

We hope *Collins Easy Learning English Conversation* will help you speak with confidence and success. For more information on products to help you improve your English, please visit us at **www.collinselt.com**.

Chatting to people

8 chatting to people

Hello

You will often want to be able to chat with people and get to know them better. The phrases in this unit will help you talk naturally to friends, family, colleagues and people that you meet in everyday situations.

Greetings

Use **Hello ...** as a general greeting. It is polite to say **hello** to anyone in any situation.

> **Hello** Jorge.

Use **Hi ...** in informal situations, for example when you are meeting friends.

> **Hi**, how's things with you?
> Oh **hi** Adam, I didn't know you were coming.

Use **Good morning**, **Good afternoon** or **Good evening** in slightly more formal situations, for instance if you meet a neighbour, or when you see people at work.

> **Good morning** everyone. Today we are going to be looking at phrasal verbs.
> **Good afternoon** Mr Kowalski.

> **GOOD TO KNOW!**
> In English, there is no greeting starting with 'Good' that is for the whole day.

Use **Goodbye ...** when you leave someone.

> **Goodbye** Clara, have a safe journey.

Goodbye ... is often shortened to **Bye ...** .

> **Bye** everyone!

Use **Goodnight ...** when you are going to bed, or if someone else is going to bed.

> **Goodnight** everyone – see you in the morning.

See you ... is a rather informal way of saying goodbye to someone you know you will see again.

> **See you** later!
> OK, I need to go now. **See you**!
> **See you** on Monday!

Introducing people

If you want to introduce someone to someone else, use **This is ...** .

> **This is** my husband, Richard.
> **This is** Medina, my friend from school.
> **These are** my children, Andrew, Gordon and Emma.

In slightly formal situations, use **I'd like you to meet ...** or **Can I introduce you to ...** ?

> **I'd like you to meet** Dr Bjornson. Dr Bjornson has been working on our project.
> **I'd like you to meet** our head of department, Anke Hub.

> **Can I introduce you to** my husband, Andre?
> **Can I introduce you to** Otto, who's going to be giving a talk later?

> **GOOD TO KNOW!**
> When you are introduced to someone, you can just say **Hello**, or in a slightly more formal situation, say **Pleased to meet you**.

Useful words
a project   a plan or piece of work that takes a lot of time and effort

Talking about yourself

When you are talking to people, you will probably want to tell them some things about you. To say what your name is, use **I'm ...** or, in a slightly more formal situation, **My name's ...** .

> Hi, **I'm** Tariq – I'm a friend of Susi.
> **I'm** Paul – I'm your teacher for this week.
>
> **My name's** Johann.
> **My name's** Yuko – I'm Kazuo's sister.

To give general information about yourself, use **I'm ...** .

> **I'm** a friend of Paolo's.
> **I'm** married with two children.
> **I'm** training for the London Marathon.

You can also give general information about yourself using **I've got ...** .

> **I've got** some friends who live in Nairobi.
> **I've got** relatives in Australia.
> **We've got** a cottage in France.

To talk about your work, use **I'm ...** with the name of a job, or **I work ...** to say something more general about what you do.

> **I'm** a doctor.
> **I'm** a bus driver.
>
> **I work** for an oil company.
> **I work** as a translator.

Useful words

a marathon	a race in which people run a distance of 26 miles (about 42 kilometres)
a relative	a member of your family
a cottage	a small house, usually in the country
a translator	someone whose job is to change words into a different language

> **GOOD TO KNOW!**
> If you want to ask someone what their job is, use **What do you do?**.

To talk about where you live, use **I live ...** or **I'm from ...** . **I'm from ...** is also used to talk about where you were born and lived as a child, even if you do not live there now.

> **I live** in Wales.
> **We live** near Moscow.
>
> **I'm from** Poland originally, but I live in Paris now.
> **We're from** Manchester.
> **My family's from** India – my parents moved here in 1970.

> **GOOD TO KNOW!**
> To ask someone where they live, use **Where do you live?** or
> **Where are you from?**.

If you are in a place for a short time, either on holiday or for work, you can say where you are living by using **I'm staying ...** .

> **I'm staying** at the Hotel Tulip.
> **I'm staying** with friends in Budapest.
> **I'm staying** in Paris for a week.

Asking for information

After saying hello to someone, especially someone you know, you usually ask about their health, by saying **How are you?** .

> Hello, Jan. **How are you**?
> It's great to see you, Anna. **How are you?**

Useful words
originally   used for talking about something that existed or was true at the beginning

chatting to people

> **GOOD TO KNOW!**
> To answer the question 'How are you?', use **I'm fine, thanks.** or **I'm good, thanks.** . If you are not well, you could say **Not great, really.** or **Not too good, actually.** .

To ask someone you know about their life in general, use **How are things (with you)?** .

> Hello, Jan. **How are things?**
> Nice to see you, Karl. **How are things with you?**

When you are chatting to someone, you will want to ask them about their life. Use **Tell me ...** for general questions.

> **Tell me** about your family.
> **Tell me** a bit about yourself.
> **Tell me** about your trip to Africa.

To ask someone to describe something, use **What's ... like?**.

> **What's** your course **like**?
> **What's** your home town **like**?
> **What's** your hotel **like**?

How's ... ? is used to ask someone's opinion of the quality of something, or whether they are enjoying it.

> **How's** your hotel?
> **How's** university?
> **How was** the concert?

A slightly informal way of asking someone about something they are doing is **How's ... going?** .

> **How's** the new job **going**?
> **How's** your project **going**?
> **How's** it **going** at college?

Saying what you want to do

When you're talking to friends or colleagues you will often need to be able to talk about what you would like to do. The simplest way is to use **I'd like to ...** .

> **I'd like to** get home early tonight.
> **I'd like to** meet your brother.

A slightly informal way of saying that you would like to do or have is **I (quite) fancy ...** or **I wouldn't mind ...** .

> **I fancy** going to a disco.
> **I quite fancy** a swim.
>
> **I wouldn't mind** going to see a film.
> **I wouldn't mind** something to eat.

> **GOOD TO KNOW!**
> **I wouldn't mind + -ing**
> The verb that comes after **I wouldn't mind ...** must be in the -ing form.

Making suggestions

One easy way of making suggestions to your friends and colleagues is to use **We could ...** .

> **We could** ask Paul to join us.
> **We could** take turns to introduce ourselves.

Useful words
take turns   to do something one after the other

14 chatting to people

If you are eager to do something with your friends or colleagues, use **Let's ...** .

> **Let's** all go bowling after work.
> **Let's** invite lots of people.
> **Let's** send invitations to all our colleagues.

If you want to make a suggestion and see if other people agree with you, use **Shall we ... ?** .

> **Shall we** see what Georgi wants to do?
> **Shall we** have a working lunch?
> **Shall we** ask Suri for her advice?
> **Shall we** go to Jordi's party this evening?

If you have an idea about something you could do, use **How about ... ?** or **What about ... ?** .

> **How about** going swimming?
> **How about** asking for some time off work?
> **How about** sending him a text?

> **What about** booking a private room?
> **What about** ordering a takeaway?
> **What about** buying her some flowers to say thank you?

> **GOOD TO KNOW!**
> **How about/What about + -ing**
> The verb that comes after **How about ... ?** or **What about ... ?**
> must be in the -ing form.

Useful words

bowling	a game in which you roll a heavy ball down a narrow track toward a group of wooden objects and try to knock down as many of them as possible
a working lunch	a meal in the middle of the day where you work at the same time as eating
private	only for one particular person or group, and not for everyone
order	to ask for something to be sent to you from a company
a takeaway	hot cooked food that you buy from a shop or a restaurant and eat somewhere else

Another way of making a suggestion to your friends and colleagues is to use **Why don't ... ?**.

> **Why don't** we get together some time?
> **Why don't** we invite Fabien and his girlfriend?
> **Why don't** you meet me for lunch?
> **Why don't** you phone them?

Expressing opinions

When talking to people in a social or work situation, you may want to express your opinion of something. The simplest way is to use **I think ...** .

> **I think** Sonia's right.
> I don't **think** Marc's coming.

You can also use **In my opinion ...** . This is a strong way to express your opinion, and is more suitable at work than with friends.

> **In my opinion**, he should be sacked.
> **In my opinion**, we need more staff.
> **In my opinion**, it's a great company to work for.

If you want to ask other people their opinion of something, use **What do you think of ... ?** or **What do you think about ... ?**.

> **What do you think of** his latest movie?
> **What do you think of** Mira's new boyfriend?

> **What do you think about** going out for dinner tonight?
> **What do you think about** inviting Eva?

To agree with someone's opinion, use **I agree**. or **You're right**. If you want to say who you agree with, use **with**.

> 'This is a great restaurant.' '**I agree**. We often come here.'
> **I agree with** Nigel.

I entirely **agree with** you!

'We'll be late if we don't hurry.' '**You're right** – let's go!'
I think **you're right**.
Matthieu**'s right**.

If you do not agree with someone, you can use **I don't agree**. This is quite strong, so to be more polite, you might say **I'm afraid I don't agree.** or **I don't really agree.**

'What a great party.' '**I don't agree**. It's much too crowded and noisy.'
'I thought Clara was really funny.' '**I'm afraid I don't agree**. I found her jokes rather offensive.'
'I think it's best not to invite children to weddings.' '**I don't really agree**. After all, weddings are all about family life.'

Talking about your plans

When talking to your colleagues and friends you will want to tell them about your plans. The simplest way is to use **I'm** followed by a verb in the **-ing** form.

I'm seeing Philippe on Thursday.
I'm having lunch with Jude.
We're getting a new computer tomorrow.

You can also use **I'm planning to ...** or, for something that you want to do, but which is not certain, **I'm hoping to ...** .

I'm planning to invite everyone I know.
I'm planning to come along later.
We're planning to open a new office in Berlin.

Useful words
crowded   full of people
offensive   rude or insulting

I'm hoping to meet her this week.
I'm hoping to be home by 10.
We're hoping to get a table at The Ivy.

Making arrangements

When you make arrangements with someone, you may want to check if they are happy with them. Use **Would it suit you ... ?** .

Would it suit you to have dinner at nine?
Would it suit you if I come round next week?
Would it suit you better if we have the meeting tomorrow?

To ask someone if they would prefer a different arrangement, use **Would you prefer it if ... ?** or **Would it be better ... ?** .

Would you prefer it if we met in town?
Would you prefer it if we ate in a restaurant?
Would you prefer it if I came to collect you?

Would it be better to postpone the meeting?
Would it be better to ring you in the evening?
Would it be better if we came a bit earlier?

A common way to agree on the time or date of an arrangement is to use **Shall we say ... ?** .

OK, **shall we say** next Thursday, then?
Lunch at Café Rouge would be great. **Shall we say** one o'clock?
I'll meet you as soon as I've finished this bit of work – **shall we say** half an hour?

Useful words

collect	to go and get someone from a place where they are waiting for you
postpone	to arrange for an event to happen at a later time

Saying what you have to do

When you want to tell your friends or colleagues that you have to do something, use **I have to ...** .

> **I have to** make a phone call.
> **We have to** be there at eight o' clock sharp.
> I really **have to** get this work finished today.
> **You** don't **have to** stay at the hotel.

To ask what someone has to do, use **Do you have to ...?** .

> **Do you have to** give them an answer today?
> **Do you have to** wait for Sam?
> **Do we have to** bring something?

To emphasize that it is necessary for you to do something, you can also use **I must ...** .

> **I must** warn them.
> I absolutely **must** finish this work today.
> **I mustn't** forget to send her an email.

When you want to say that you should do something, use **I should ...** or **I ought to ...** .

> **I should** try to book tickets.
> **You should** come and visit us.
> **I shouldn't** stay much longer.

> **I ought to** check that Roma's OK.
> **I ought to** book a taxi.
> **We ought to** check their website.

Useful words

sharp	at that exact time
warn	to tell someone about something such as a possible danger
legal	relating to the law
book	to arrange to have or use something, such as a hotel room or a ticket to a concert, at a later time

chatting to people

● Listen out for

Here are some useful phrases which you may hear or want to use in conversation.

> Have you ever been to Berlin?
> How long are you staying in Rouen?
> How long have you been learning English?
> Your English is very good.
> Am I speaking too fast?
> Would you prefer it if I spoke German?
> Are you married?
> Have you got any children?
> Do you come here often?
> What do you do in your spare time?
> Are you enjoying living here?
> Have you worked here for a long time?
> Could you speak a bit slower, please?
>
> Thank you for inviting me – I've had a lovely time.
> I hope we'll meet again some time.
> Thank you for a lovely evening.
> What a lovely party!
> I've had a great time, thanks.

Listen to the conversation: Track 1

Brett has just started working at a hospital in Oxford. He is meeting one of his colleagues, Jim, for the first time.

A Hi, I'm Jim. I hear you've just started work here. I hope you'll enjoy it.

B Pleased to meet you. Which department are you in?

A I'm one of the physiotherapists.

B How long have you been working here?

A Nearly eight years now. I'm from Yorkshire originally. How about you? Where are you from?

B I'm from Australia – Perth, right over on the west.

A Really? I've got relatives in Canberra – I love Australia! Where are you living at the moment?

B I'm staying at a hotel, but I'm hoping to get a flat near the hospital, if things work out well. What's it like, working here?

A Pretty good. It's a friendly place. In fact, I'd like you to meet the rest of my team some time. We usually meet up for a meal on Fridays – why don't you join us?

B That would be great, thanks.

A Would next Friday suit you?

B Sure. I don't know anyone yet, so I'm free every night!

A OK, shall we say 8 o'clock, at the Golden Curry?

B Sounds good. See you then!

 Listen to more phrases and practise saying them: Track 2

Travelling

Have a good trip!

If you are travelling, these phrases will help you to find out how to get to places and do things such as buy tickets. They will also help you to talk about travelling in clear, natural English.

Talking about your plans

Use **I'm + -ing verb ...** or **I'm going to ...** to talk about travel plans that you are sure of.

> **I'm spending** a couple of days in Paris on the way back.
> **They're going** on a package holiday this summer, as usual.
> **I'm having** a stopover in Thailand on the way there.

> **I'm going to** do a course in London.
> **I'm going to** travel first-class.
> **I'm going to** go travelling this summer.

Use **Are you going to ... ?** or **Will you ... ?** to ask someone about their travel plans.

> **Are you going to** travel with Tahir?
> **Are you going to** fly there?
> **Are you going to** see Sophia while you're in Milan?

> **Will you** manage to do any sightseeing in between meetings?
> **Will you** charge us extra for the bigger room?
> **Will you** call me when you get to your hotel?

Useful words

a couple	two or around two people or things
a package holiday	a holiday in which the flight and hotels are arranged by one travel company and are included in the price that you pay to that company
a stopover	a stop during a flight
first-class	used for describing the best and most expensive seats on a train or in an aeroplane

To talk about your travel plans, you can also use **I'm planning to ...** or, if you are slightly less sure, **I'm hoping to ...** .

I'm planning to spend a few days in Berlin.
We're planning to drive along the coast.
Jack and Millie are planning to come over this year.

I'm hoping to stay in youth hostels most of the time.
She's hoping to do a tour of the nearby islands.
We're hoping to fit in some skiing while we're in the mountains.

To talk about a travel plan that is only possible, use **I might ...** .

I might book a hotel for that night.
I might spend an extra week in Calgary.
I might stay on if I like it there.

To talk about something that should happen in the future, use **I'm supposed to ...** .

I'm supposed to be at the station by 8:00.
I'm supposed to be meeting Brett in Paris.
What time **are we supposed to** get there?
He's supposed to be driving me to the airport.

Useful words

sightseeing	the activity of travelling around, visiting the interesting places that tourists usually visit
charge	to ask someone to pay money for something
coast	the land that is next to the sea
a youth hostel	a cheap hotel where a traveller can stay for one or two nights
a tour	a trip to an interesting place or around several interesting places
an island	a piece of land that is completely surrounded by water
fit in	to find the time to do something
book	to arrange to have something, such as a hotel room, at a later time
stay on	to remain in a place for more time than you intended

Saying what you have to do

If it is important for you to do something, such as buy a ticket or catch a train, use **I have to ...** or **I need to ...** .

> **I have to** be at the airport at seven.
> **I have to** take the local train to Niort first.
> **We have to** be there by 8 o'clock.
> I'm going to get to the station early as **I have to** buy my ticket.

> **I need to** book a bed and breakfast.
> **I need to** change trains at Birmingham.
> **I need to** call the hotel and book an extra room.
> **We need to** call a taxi.

Another way of saying that it is important that you do something is **I must ...** . This is used especially when it is *very* important that you do something.

> **I must** collect the car before three.
> **I must** remember to take my passport.
> **I must** change my flight.
> **You must** print out your e-ticket and take it with you.

> **GOOD TO KNOW!**
> **must + infinitive**
> The verb that comes after **must ...** is in the infinitive form without 'to'.

Useful words

local	in, or relating to, the area where you live
a bed and breakfast	a small hotel in which you get a room for the night and a meal in the morning
collect	to go and get someone or something from a place where they are waiting for you
a passport	an official document that you have to show when you enter or leave a country
print out	to use a machine to produce a copy of a computer file on paper
an e-ticket	a ticket for a flight or train journey that is in electronic form

Saying what you want to do

The simplest way to say that you want to do something such as buy a ticket or catch a train is to use **I'd like to ...** . If you know that you do not want to do something, use **I don't want to ...** .

> **I'd like to** hire a bike.
> **I'd like to** make a reservation.
> Good morning, **I'd like to** book a double room.

> **I don't want to** spend too much on accommodation.
> **I don't want to** leave my luggage at the hotel.
> **I don't want to** get stuck in the traffic.

If you are very eager to do something, use **I'd really like to ...** or **I'd love to ...** .

> **I'd really like to** get there early.
> **I'd really like to** travel back with Julia.

> **I'd love to** travel as a part of my job.
> **I'd love to** see the north of the country.

Use **I'd rather ...** when you want to do one thing and not another. If you want to mention the thing that you do not want, you should use **than** before it.

> **I'd rather** take the earlier flight.
> **We'd rather** stay in a B&B.
> **I'd rather** be nearer the town centre **than** stay somewhere out of the city.

Useful words

hire	to pay to use something, such as a car, for a short time
a reservation	a room or a seat that a hotel, a transport company or a restaurant keeps ready for you
a double room	a room in a hotel that is intended for two people
accommodation	buildings or rooms where people live or stay
luggage	the bags that you take with you when you travel
stuck	unable to move
traffic	all the vehicles that are on a particular road at one time
B&B	a bed and breakfast; a small hotel in which you get a room for the night and a meal in the morning

Making suggestions

The simplest way to make a travel suggestion is to say **We could ...** or **Shall we ... ?**.

> **We could** take a taxi instead.
> **We could** travel overnight.

> **Shall we** walk there?
> **Shall we** leave our bags here?

Another way to make a travel suggestion is to say **Why don't ... ?** or **Why not ... ?**.

> **Why don't** we hitchhike to the coast?
> **Why don't** you buy a ticket online?

> **Why not** see if Umar can take us?
> **Why not** ask Dad if he can drive you to the airport?

Use **How about ... ?** if you have an idea about, for example, where to stay or how to get somewhere.

> **How about** seeing if a bed and breakfast in the town centre has any vacancies?
> **How about** asking Maria to give you a lift?

> **GOOD TO KNOW!**
> **How about + -ing**
> The verb that comes after **How about ... ?** must be in the -ing form.

Useful words

overnight	happening through the whole night or at some point during the night
hitchhike	to travel by getting rides from passing vehicles without paying
online	using the Internet
a vacancy	when a room in a hotel is empty
a lift	when you take someone somewhere in your car

Asking for information

You may need to go to a particular place or building when you are travelling. Use **Is there ... ?** to ask if there is such a place or building where you are. You may need to get someone's attention before you can ask them a question. Use **Excuse me** to do this.

> Excuse me, **is there** a café in this station?
> Excuse me, **is there** an underground station near here?
> Excuse me, **are there** any restaurants around here?
> Excuse me, **are there** any public toilets near here?

Another way to ask this question is **Where can I find ... ?**.

> Excuse me, **where can I find** a tourist information office?
> Excuse me, **where can I find** information about local bus services?
> Excuse me, **where can I find** a train timetable?

You could use **I'm looking for ...** to get the same information.

> Excuse me, **I'm looking for** the nearest underground station.
> Excuse me, **I'm looking for** the town centre.
> Excuse me, **I'm looking for** the train station.

You can also ask the same question by starting your sentence with **Do you know ... ?** .

> Excuse me, **do you know** where there's a petrol station?
> Excuse me, **do you know** where I can find the tourist information office?
> Excuse me, **do you know** where the ticket office is?

Useful words

the underground	in a city, the railway system in which electric trains travel below the ground in tunnels
a public toilet	a toilet in a place where everyone can use it
a timetable	a list of the times when trains, buses or planes arrive and depart
a petrol station	a place where you can buy fuel for your car

If you want someone to suggest something that might be useful to you while you are away, use **Can you recommend ... ?**.

> **Can you recommend** a hotel in the town centre?
> **Can you recommend** a tour guide?

Use **Can you give me the number ... ?** to ask for the phone number of someone who can provide a service for you while you are travelling.

> **Can you give me the number** of a local dentist?
> **Can you give me the number** of a taxi service?

While you are travelling, you may want to find out the way to do something, for example how to buy a ticket. Use **How do ... ?**.

> Excuse me, **how do** I buy a ticket from this machine?
> **How do** I use this phone?
> **How do** I call a number in Germany?
> **How do** we get to the station?

Use **Can I ... ?** to ask if you are allowed to do something.

> **Can I** buy a ticket on the train?
> **Can I** leave my bags here?
> **Can I** change my ticket if I need to?
> **Can I** pay by credit card?

If you want to know the time that something happens, ask **What time ... ?**.

> **What time** does the train leave?
> **What time** do we get to Brussels?
> **What time** do we arrive in Portland?
> **What time** are we boarding?

Useful words

a tour guide	someone whose job is to help people who are on holiday, or to show them round a place
a credit card	a plastic card that you use to buy something and pay for it later
board	to get into a train, a ship or an aircraft to travel somewhere

If you want to ask how much time something takes, use **How long ... ?**.

> **How long** is the flight?
> **How long** does the journey take?
> **How long** will it take us to walk there?
> **How long** is the crossing?

If you want to ask how many times something happens, **How often do ... ?**.

> **How often do** the trains go?
> **How often do** the trains to Cambridge go?
> **How often do** the buses to Oxford go?

If you want to ask about the money that you need to do something, use **How much ... ?**.

> **How much** is a ticket to Amsterdam?
> **How much** is a return ticket?
> **How much** does it cost to fly there?
> **How much** does it cost to hire a car?

Asking for things

If you want to ask for something while you are travelling, the simplest way is to use **Can I have ... ?** or **Could I have ... ?**. To be polite, use **please** at the beginning or end.

> **Can I have** an aisle seat, please?
> **Can I have** a train timetable, please?

Useful words

a journey	an occasion when you travel from one place to another
a crossing	a journey across a river or sea
a return ticket	a ticket for a journey to a place and back again
an aisle	a long, narrow passage where people can walk between rows of seats

Could I have a ticket to Palm Beach, please?
Could I have a weekly pass, please?

If you want to find out if something is available, use **Do you have ... ?**.

Excuse me, **do you have** a lost property office?
Excuse me, **do you have** a non-smoking area?

If you are asking someone whether they can do something for you, use **Can you ... ?** or **Could you ... ?**. **Could you ... ?** is slightly more polite and formal than **Can you ... ?**. To be polite, use **please** at the beginning or end of these sentences.

Can you help me, please?
Can you let me out here, please?

Could you give me directions to the town centre, please?
Could you write down the address for me, please?

A very polite way to ask someone if they will do something for you is **Would you mind ... ?** or **Do you mind ... ?**.

Would you mind writing down the address for me?
Would you mind dropping me at my hotel?

Do you mind marking the hotel on this map?
Do you mind looking after my bag while I go to the toilet, please?

Useful words

weekly	for one week, or happening every week
a pass	a document that allows you to do something
a lost-property office	a place where things are kept that people have lost or accidentally left in public places
non-smoking	where smoking is not allowed
directions	instructions that tell you how to get somewhere
write something down	to record something on a piece of paper using a pen or a pencil
drop	to take someone somewhere in a car and leave them there
look after someone/something	to take care of someone or something

> **GOOD TO KNOW!**
> **Would/Do you mind + -ing**
> The verb that comes after **Would/Do you mind ... ?** must be in the -ing form.

Use **Could I ... ?** or **May I ... ?** when you want to ask if you can do something.

Could I collect my luggage, please?
Could I check in, please?
Could I leave my bags here, please?

May I use your phone?
May I sit here?
May I put my bag here?

Saying what you like, dislike, prefer

You may want to talk about what you like and do not like about travelling. The simplest way to say that you like something is to use **I like ...** . To say that you like doing an activity, use **I enjoy ...** . To ask someone if they like or enjoy something, use **Do you like ... ?** or **Do you enjoy ... ?**.

I like travelling on the the high-speed trains.
Do you like driving or being driven?

I enjoy just looking out of the window.
Do you enjoy exploring new places?

Useful words

check in	to tell the person at the desk of an airport or a hotel that you have arrived
high-speed	fast
explore	to travel around a place to find out what it is like

If you want to say that you like something very much, use **I really like ...** or **I love ...** .

> **I really like** these country roads.
> **I really like** travelling because you get to see a different way of life.

> **I love** looking at the scenery from the train.
> I'm very happy when I'm travelling but I also **love** coming home.

To say that you do not like something, use **I don't like ...** , or to say that you *really* do not like something, use **I hate ...** .

> **I don't like** flying.
> **I don't like** carrying a backpack.

> **I hate** getting stuck in traffic.
> **I hate** long-haul flights.

If you want to say that you like one thing more than another thing, use **I prefer ...** . To talk about the thing that you like less, use **to** before it.

> **I prefer** going on the train **to** driving.
> I do travel on my own but **I prefer** travelling with other people.

Useful words

scenery	the land, water or plants that you can see around you in a country area
a backpack	a bag that you carry on your back
a long-haul flight	a flight over a long distance

● Listen out for

Here are some important phrases you are likely to hear and use when you are travelling about.

Could I see your tickets, please?
Could you have your tickets ready, please?
This is the 5:45 to London, stopping at Finsbury Park only.
A return ticket to Portland, please.
A single ticket to Glasgow, please.
Change at Oxford for Slough.
The train for Nice leaves from platform three.
Do you mind if I sit here?
Passengers are reminded to take all their personal belongings with them when they leave the train.

Flight 208 is now boarding from gate 12.
Passengers are reminded that smoking is not allowed anywhere on the plane.
Please store all bags in the overhead lockers.

Go straight on till you get to the traffic lights.
Carry on down this road.
Take the second turning on the left.
It's opposite the cathedral.
You can walk there.
It's too far to walk.
It will take you ten minutes to walk there.
It's three stops from here.

Useful words

Do you mind ... ?	used to ask someone if you can do something
remind	to say something that makes someone remember to do something
belongings	the things that you own
overhead	above you
a locker	a small cupboard with a lock
straight on	continuing in one direction
carry on	to continue to do something

Listen to the conversation: Track 3

Emma is telling her colleague Jim about her travel plans.

A So what are your plans for this summer?

B I've decided I'm going to go travelling with my friend, Ashley.

A Really, where are you going?

B We're thinking we'd like to explore Northern Europe – Sweden and Norway and we're hoping to get to Denmark too.

A Will you fly there?

B No, we both hate flying. We're planning to do it all by boat and train.

A Really? I'd always rather fly. It's so much quicker and more convenient.

B Not me, I prefer trains and boats – they're so much more relaxing. I like sitting back and enjoying the scenery. And, of course, they're better for the environment.

A Will you go to Stockholm?

B I hope so. Do you know it?

A Yes, I spent a summer there as part of my studies – it's possibly my favourite city in the world. You absolutely must go there.

B Well, we'll make sure we do then! Do you have a travel guide for Stockholm, by any chance?

A I do – a good one.

B Would you mind lending it to me for the summer?

A Sure. I'll bring it with me the next time we meet for coffee.

B And what about you? Are you going to get away this summer?

A I don't know – work is going to be very busy over the next few months. I might manage a weekend break somewhere – perhaps France. I'll have to see how it goes.

B You like France, don't you?

A Very much. I really like the way of life there. I sometimes think I'd like to live in France. Anyway, I'd better go now. I'm supposed to be meeting Enrique in town in ten minutes.

B Okay, bye!

A Bye, Emma!

 Listen to more phrases and practise saying them: Track 4

Where we live

Make yourself at home!

The phrases in this unit will help you to talk about your accommodation. You can use them if you are trying to find a hotel, if you are looking for somewhere to live, or if you want to talk about the place where you live.

Asking for things

To say what kind of place you want, either in a hotel or if you want to rent or buy a place to live, use **I'd like ...** .

> **I'd like** a double room.
> **I'd like** to rent a cottage in the mountains.
> **I'd like** a ground floor flat.
> **I'd like** an en-suite room.

To talk about the kind of place you want, use **I'm looking for ...** .

> **I'm looking for** a room in a shared house.
> **I'm looking for** cheap accommodation in the area.
> **I'm looking for** a place to rent.
> **We're looking for** a house with four bedrooms and a garage.

GOOD TO KNOW!
Accommodation is one of the words most often spelled wrong in English. Remember that it has **cc** and **mm**.

Useful words

accommodation	buildings or rooms where people live or stay
a double room	a room for two people
rent	to pay the owner of something in order to be able to use it yourself
a cottage	a small house, usually in the country
en-suite	with a bathroom attached
the ground floor	the part of a building that is at the same level as the ground
a garage	a building where you keep a car

To explain to someone what you want, use **I want ...** .

>**I want** a house with a large garden.
>**I want** to rent a house for six months.
>**I wanted** a bigger kitchen.
>**We don't want** to live in the suburbs.

If you are in a hotel and you need something, use **Could I have ... ?** .

>**Could I have** the key to my room, please?
>**Could I have** a receipt, please?
>**Could I have** an extra pillow, please?
>**Could we have** some more towels?

To make sure that a hotel has everything you need, use **Do you have ... ?** .

>**Do you have** internet access?
>**Do you have** a gym?
>**Do you have** any family rooms?
>**Do you have** conference facilities?

To ask someone to do something for you, use **Could you ... ?** .

>**Could you** ask the landlord to fix the heating?
>**Could you** let me know if any similar houses come on the market?
>**Could you** call a taxi for me, please?
>**Could you** tell me how far it is from the station?

Useful words

a suburb	one of the areas on the edge of a city where many people live
a receipt	a piece of paper that shows that you have paid for something
a pillow	a soft object that you rest your head on when you are in bed
access	when you are able to use equipment
a gym	a large room with equipment for doing physical exercises
a conference	a long meeting about a particular subject
facilities	something such as rooms, buildings or pieces of equipment that are used for a particular purpose
a landlord	a man who owns a building and allows people to live there in return for rent

Asking for information

When you want to obtain some information about your accommodation, the most simple way is to start your question with **Is ... ?** .

Is it near the university?
Is it a luxury hotel?
Is the flat available immediately?
Is breakfast included in the price?
Are the bills included in the rent?

You could also use **Could you tell me ... ?** or **I'd like to know ...** .

Could you tell me what the neighbourhood is like?
Could you tell me if there are any laundry facilities?
Could you tell me what the monthly rent is?

I'd like to know if the hotel has a swimming pool.
I'd like to know how much a double room would be.
I'd like to know whether you have any three-bedroom houses to rent.

To ask if a place has something, use **Is there ... ?**, or **Does ... have ... ?** .

Is there an ironing board in the room?
Is there an intercom?
Are there any spare pillows in the cupboard?
Are there any rules about having guests to stay?

Useful words

luxury	being pleasant and expensive
a bill	a document that shows how much you must pay for something
a neighbourhood	one of the parts of a town where people live
laundry	clothes and other things that need to be washed
an ironing board	a narrow surface like a table that you use for ironing
an intercom	a system used for communicating with people in different parts of a building, especially people who come to your door

Does the flat **have** central heating?
Does the hotel **have** a car park?
Does it **have** a patio?
Does it **have** a garage?

To ask what something is like, use **What's ... like?** .

What's your accommodation **like**?
What's the area **like** for shopping?
What's the mattress **like** on your bed?

Use **Where ... ?** to ask about where things are.

Where's the laundry room?
Where's the nearest railway station?
Where can I plug my laptop in?

To ask about time, use **What time ... ?** .

What time's breakfast?
What time is the estate agent coming?
What time do we have to leave in the morning?

To ask about prices, use **How much ... ?** .

How much is a family room?
How much do you pay your cleaner?
How much do you charge for breakfast?

Useful words

central heating	a heating system that uses hot air or water to heat every part of a building
a patio	a flat area next to a house, where people can sit and relax or eat
plug something in	to connect a piece of electrical equipment to the electricity supply
an estate agent	a person whose job is to sell buildings or land

If you want to ask someone's advice about your accommodation, use **Can you give me some advice ... ?**. Use the prepositions **about** or **on** after this phrase.

> **Can you give me some advice about** how to choose an estate agent?
> **Can you give me some advice on** the best areas to look for a flat?
> **Can you give me some advice about** having lodgers?

To ask someone about the best thing to do, use **Would you recommend ... ?**.

> **Would you recommend** hiring a builder to do the work?
> **Would you recommend** buying a place myself?
> **Would you recommend** that hotel?

> **GOOD TO KNOW!**
> **Would you recommend + -ing verb**
> When **Would you recommend** is followed by a verb, it must be in the -ing form.

Asking for permission

If you are staying in a hotel or renting somewhere to live, you may need to ask for permission. You can use **Can I ...** .

> **Can I** park outside?
> **Can I** leave my suitcases here for five minutes?
> **Can we** use the pool?
> **Can we** camp here?
> **Can we** stay another night?
> **Can we** have pets in the flat?

Useful words

a lodger	someone who pays to live in someone else's house
camp	to stay somewhere in a tent
a pet	an animal that you keep in your home

To check if you can do something, use **Am I allowed to ... ?**.

>
> **Am I allowed to** use the washing machine?
> **Am I allowed to** have guests?
> **Are we allowed to** bring our dog?

To make sure you will not upset someone, use **Do you mind if ... ?** .

>
> **Do you mind if** I keep my bike in the shed?
> **Do you mind if** I use the washing machine?
> **Do you mind if** we have a party at the weekend?

You can also use **Is it OK to ... ?** This is slightly informal.

>
> **Is it OK to** bring some of my own furniture?
> **Is it OK to** turn the heating on?
> **Is it OK to** paint the walls in my room?

Saying what you like, dislike, prefer

When you are looking for accommodation, you will probaby need to explain what you like or do not like. The simplest phrase to use is **I like ...** .

>
> **I like** modern architecture.
> I really **like** campsites in the mountains.
> I quite **like** living in the countryside.
> **I don't like** this wallpaper.
> **We don't like** living in a flat.

Useful words

a shed	a small building where you store things
architecture	the style of the design of a building
a campsite	a place where you can stay in a tent
wallpaper	coloured or patterned paper that is used for decorating the walls of rooms

If you want to say that you like one thing more than another, use **I prefer ...** .
If you want to talk about the thing you like less, use **to** before it.

> **I prefer** wooden floors to carpets.
> **I prefer** to rent, rather than buying a place.
> **I prefer** living on my own.
> **I prefer** blinds to curtains.

To say what you would prefer to do, use **I'd rather ...** . If you want to talk about
the thing you would not like to do, use **than**.

> **I'd rather** employ a cleaner.
> **I'd rather** share a flat **than** live on my own.
> **We'd rather** have the loft converted **than** move to another house.

If you would prefer not to do something, use **I'd prefer not to ...** or **I'd rather
not ...** .

> **I'd prefer not to** share a flat.
> **I'd prefer not to** stay in a hotel.
> **I'd prefer not to** spend too much money.

> **I'd rather not** live too far from my parents.
> **I'd rather not** have to do much decorating.
> **I'd rather not** have lodgers.

> **GOOD TO KNOW!**
> **I'd rather not + infinitive**
> The verb that follows **I'd rather not** must be in the infinitive form,
> without 'to'.

Useful words

a blind	a piece of cloth or other material that you can pull down over a window to cover it
employ	to pay someone to work for a person or a company
a loft	the space directly under the roof of a building
convert	to change something into a different form
decorate	to put new paint or paper on the walls or ceiling of a room

Talking about your plans

If you have decided what you are going to do, you could use **I'm going to ...** or **I'm planning to ...** .

>   **I'm going to** buy a house nearer to my work.
>   **I'm going to** stay in a hotel while the building work is going on.
>   **We're going to** camp.

>   **I'm planning to** get an architect to design the extension.
>   **I'm planning to** paint the walls yellow.
>   **I'm planning to** take a couple of lodgers.

You can also use **I'll ...** to say what you are going to do.

>   **I'll** be at the hotel at five pm.
>   **I'll** probably rent a flat at first.
>   **We'll** be there by seven.

To talk about something that you would like to do but are not sure if it is possible, use **I'm hoping to ...** .

>   **I'm hoping to** find a flat with a spare bedroom.
>   **I'm hoping to** move to Italy in the spring.
>   **I'm hoping to** find someone to share a house with me.

I intend to ... is a rather strong and definite way of talking about your plans.

>   **I intend to** rent a flat.
>   **I intend to** sell my house.
>   **I intend to** stay until Friday.

Useful words
an architect   a person whose job is to design buildings
an extension   an extra part that is added to a building to make it bigger

Complaining

Unfortunately, you may need to complain to the hotel staff or to your landlord or landlady. To talk about something that is upsetting you, use **There's ...**, and for something you think is missing, use **There isn't ...** .

> **There's** mould in the bathroom.
> **There's** a leak in the ceiling.
> **There are** mice under the floorboards.

> **There isn't** any hot water.
> **There isn't** a proper lock on the door.
> **There aren't** any clean towels in the room.

If something is not good enough, use **I'm not happy with ...** or **I'm disappointed with ...** .

> **I'm not happy with** the parking arrangements.
> **I'm not happy with** the food.
> **I'm not happy with** my room.

> **I'm disappointed with** the view.
> **I'm disappointed with** the standard of the food.
> **I'm disappointed with** the neighbourhood.

To say that you think something is bad, use **I think ...** .

> **I think** the beds are really uncomfortable.
> **I think** the rooms are cold and draughty.
> **I don't think** the rooms are cleaned often enough.

Useful words

mould	a soft grey or green substance that grows on old food or damp surfaces
a leak	when liquid or gas escapes from something
a floorboard	a long, narrow piece of wood that makes part of a floor in a building
draughty	having streams of cold air

● Listen out for

Here are some useful phrases you may hear when you are finding somewhere to stay or live.

What type of accommodation are you looking for?
Whose name is the booking in?
For how many nights?
For how many people?
Breakfast is included in the price.
Can I see your passport, please?
I'm afraid we're full.
We still have a few vacancies for that night.
There's a 300 euro deposit.
You need to give two months notice when you want to leave.
What number can we contact you on?
We don't allow dogs.
How would you like to pay?
Please fill in this form.
Please sign here.
Can you spell your name for me, please?
Would you like an alarm call?
How would you like to pay?

Useful words

a booking	an arrangement to have a hotel room, tickets, etc. at a particular time in the future
a deposit	a sum of money that is part of the full price of something, and that you pay when you agree to buy it
notice	a warning that something will happen
a vacancy	a room that is still available
an alarm call	a telephone call to wake you up in the morning

Listen to the conversation: Track 5

Emma and Brett have met for a coffee in their lunch break. Emma is explaining why she wants to move out of her flat.

A I'm trying to find a new flat, closer to work. I'm not happy with the place where I am at the moment.

B Why's that? Isn't it nice?

A Not really. It's very expensive and quite small. It doesn't have a spare room, so if I have friends to stay, they have to sleep on the sofa. Also, the facilities aren't very good. There's no washing machine, and the fridge and cooker are very old and don't work very well.

B So have you started looking for somewhere new?

A Yeah. I have to give my landlord a month's notice, so I'm hoping to find somewhere by then. I'm trying to decide which area to go for – would you recommend living in the city centre?

B Well, I love it because I go out a lot, but it's quite noisy. It depends what you like.

A I'd probably prefer somewhere a bit quieter, but I'd like to be nearer the centre.

B I'm sure you could find something nice near the centre. I've got a friend who lives near the river. I'll ring her and ask her what it's like there.

A Thanks. I was wondering about trying there.

Listen to more phrases and practise saying them: Track 6

Eating with friends

Enjoy your meal!

If you are going out for a meal, you will need to make arrangements with your friends about when and where to meet. You will also want to order food and perhaps tell your friends what food you like and do not like. The phrases in this unit will help you to do all this with confidence.

Making arrangements

When you make arrangements with someone, you may want to check if they are happy with them. Use **Would it suit you ... ?**.

> **Would it suit you** to have dinner in town?
> **Would it suit you** if I met you at the restaurant?
> **Would it suit you** better if we ate earlier?

To ask someone if they would prefer a different arrangement, use **Would you prefer it if ... ?** or **Would it be better ... ?**.

> **Would you prefer it if** we went to the Italian restaurant near you?
> **Would you prefer it if** we didn't invite Claudia?
> **Would you prefer it if** we postponed having dinner till next week?

> **Would it be better** to book a table in advance?
> **Would it be better** to go to a restaurant that we know?
> **Would it be better** if we ate out somewhere?

To make sure someone is happy with a plan, use **Is ... OK?**.

> **Is** seven o'clock for dinner **OK** or is that too early for you?
> I was thinking of the Greek restaurant on Southbourne Street. **Is** that **OK** with you?

Useful words

suit	to be convenient for you
postpone	to arrange for an event to happen at a later time
book	to arrange to have or use something, such as a hotel room or a table in a restaurant, at a later time
in advance	before a particular date or event
eat out	to eat in a restaurant

Is it **OK** if I get to the restaurant a bit later?
Is it **OK** to meet in the restaurant?

Another way to make sure that someone is happy with a plan is to use **How does ... sound?**.

I was thinking we'd meet for dinner and then see a film. **How does** that **sound**?
What about dinner at 8:00 in Franco's. **How does** that **sound**?
What about a snack in The Book Shop café, followed by shopping. **How does** that **sound**?
How does eight-thirty for dinner **sound**?

A common way to agree on the time or date of arrangement is to use **Shall we say ... ?**.

So what time are we meeting at the restaurant? **Shall we say** eight o'clock – or is that too late?
Lunch at Café Otto sounds cool. **Shall we say** one o'clock inside the café?
Shall we say twelve-thirty in the restaurant? Is that okay?
Shall we say seven o'clock for dinner? Does that suit you?

Asking for information

Use **Is ... ?** to ask general questions about the food that is on the menu.

Is the pasta dish vegetarian?
Is the sauce hot?

Useful words

a snack	a simple meal that is quick to prepare and to eat
cool	convenient
a menu	a list of the food and drink that you can have in a restaurant
pasta	a type of food made from a mixture of flour, eggs and water that is made into different shapes
vegetarian	not containing meat or fish
sauce	a thick liquid that you eat with other food.
hot	having a strong, burning taste

Is this dish spicy?
Is that a type of meat?

Use **What is ... ?** to ask about a particular dish.

What is "gravy"?
What is "jelly"?
What is that on your plate?

Use **What's in ... ?** to ask about the foods that are in a particular dish.

What's in this dish?
What's in a "cassoulet"?
Can I ask **what's in** this dish?

Use **Is there any ... ?** or **Are there any ... ?** to ask whether a particular food is in a dish.

Is there any milk in this?
Is there any alcohol in this?
Are there any nuts in this dish?
Are there any bones in the fish?

Useful words

spicy	strongly flavoured with spices
gravy	a sauce that is made from the juices that come from meat when it cooks
jelly	a soft sweet food made from fruit juice and sugar that moves from side to side when you touch it
alcohol	a liquid that is found in drinks such as beer and wine
a nut	a dry fruit with a hard shell
a bone	one of the hard white parts inside a person or animal's body

Asking for things

When you arrive at the restaurant, you will want to tell the waiter or waitress how many people will be eating so they can find the right size table for you. Use **A table for ... please**.

>**A table for** two, **please**.
>'**A table for** six, **please**.' 'Certainly, Sir. Come this way.'

In most restaurants someone will soon come to your table to take your order. To say which dish you want, use **I'd like ...** or **I'll have ...** . To be polite, use **please** after this.

>**I'd like** the Margarita pizza, please.
>For my starter, **I'd like** the salad, please.
>For my main course, **I'd like** the pasta.
>For dessert, **I'd like** ice-cream.

>**I'll have** the lamb, please.
>**I'll have** the fish soup as a starter, please.
>For dessert, **I'll have** the fruit.
>**We'll have** water to drink.

>**GOOD TO KNOW!**
>If the waiter or waitress comes to your table to take your order and you have not decided what to choose, say **We haven't decided yet**. or **Could you come back in five minutes, please?**.

Useful words

an order	the thing that someone has asked for
a starter	a small amount of food that you eat as the first part of a meal
a salad	a mixture of food, usually vegetables, that you usually serve cold
a main course	the biggest part of a meal
a dessert	something sweet that you eat at the end of a meal
lamb	the flesh of a lamb, eaten as food
soup	a liquid food made by boiling meat, fish or vegetables in water

To ask if something is available, use **Do you have ... ?**.

> **Do you have** a children's menu?
> **Do you have** a table outside?

If the waiter or waitress has brought food to your table but you need something else, use **Can I have ... ?** or **Could I have ... ?**. To be polite, use **please** at the beginning or end of the question.

> **Can I have** the dessert menu, please?
> **Can I have** some pepper, please?
> **Can I have** some ketchup, please?

> **Can I have** another fork, please?
> **Could I have** some water, please?
> **Could I have** the bill, please?

If you are asking someone if they can do something for you, use **Can you ... ?** or **Could you ... ?**. **Could you ... ?** is slightly more polite and formal than **Can you ... ?**.

> **Can you** pass me the salt, please?
> Please **can you** bring us another glass?

> **Could you** bring us our coffee, please?
> **Could you** bring us the bill, please?

Useful words

pepper	a spice with a hot taste that you put on food
ketchup	a thick red sauce made from tomatoes
a fork	a tool with long metal points used for eating food
pass	to give an object to someone
the bill	a document that shows how much money you must pay for something

A polite way of asking someone to do something is by saying **Would you mind ... ?** .

> **Would you mind** taking our order?
> **Would you mind** bringing us some salt?

To ask whether something you want is possible, use **Is it possible to ... ?**

> **Is it possible to** change our order?
> **Is it possible to** have this dish as a starter?

Saying what you want to do

To say what you want to do, use **I'd like to ...** . If you are very eager to do something, use **I'd really like to ...** or **I'd love to ...** .

> **I'd like to** eat a little earlier.
> **I'd like to** have fish tonight.

> **I'd really like to** try that new Spanish restaurant on Green Street.
> **I'd really like to** eat there again.

> **I'd love to** have one of their desserts.
> **I'd love to** take Carlos to that restaurant.

Use **I'd rather ...** when you want to do one thing and not another. If you want to mention the thing that you do not want, you should use **than** before it.

> **I'd rather** eat later, if that's possible.
> **I'd rather** eat in the hotel **than** go out to a restaurant.

Useful words
salt   a white substance that you use to improve the flavour of food

Saying what you like, dislike, prefer

When you are eating in a restaurant, you may like to talk about the food that you like and do not like. The simplest way to talk about things you like is to use **I like ...** . To talk about activities that you like doing, use **I enjoy ...** .

> **I like** all kinds of cheese.
> **I like** most vegetables.
> **Do you like** spicy food?

> **I enjoy** eating out with friends.
> I really **enjoy** going to new restaurants.
> **Do you enjoy** trying different sorts of food?

> **GOOD TO KNOW!**
> **Like/Enjoy + -ing**
> When **like ...** or **enjoy ...** is followed by a verb, the verb is usually in the -ing form.

If you like something, but not in a strong way, use **I quite like ...** .

> **I quite like** ice-cream.
> **I quite like** burgers.

If you like something very much, you can say **I really like ...** or **I love ...** .

> **I really like** Indian food.
> **I really like** meat.

> **I love** seafood.
> **I love** desserts.

Useful words

spicy	strongly flavoured with spices
a burger	meat that is cut into very small pieces and pressed into a flat, round shape, often eaten between two slices of bread
seafood	fish and other small animals from the sea that you can eat

eating with friends

To tell someone that you do not like a food, use **I don't like ...** .

> **I don't like** olives.
> **I don't like** fast food.

To ask someone if they do not like a particular food, use **Don't you like ... ?**.

> **Don't you like** sweet food?
> **Don't you like** chocolate?

To say very strongly that you do not like a food, use **I hate ...** .

> **I hate** mushrooms.
> **She hates** tomatoes.

If you want to say that you like one food more than another, use **I prefer ...** .
If you want to talk about the food you like less, use **to** before it.

> I don't really like meat. **I prefer** fish.
> **I prefer** my mum's food **to** any restaurant food.

To talk about something that you do not like to do, use **I prefer not to ...** .

> **I prefer not to** eat late at night.
> **She prefers not to** eat too much rich food.

Useful words

an olive	a small green or black fruit with a bitter taste
fast food	hot food that is served quickly in a restaurant
a mushroom	a plant with a short stem and a round part that you can eat
rich	containing a lot of butter, eggs or cream

Asking for suggestions

If you want to ask the waiter or other people at your table to tell you about something that is good to eat, use **Can you recommend ... ?** or **What do you recommend ... ?**.

> **Can you recommend** a drink to go with our meal?
> **Can you recommend** a local dish?
> **Can you recommend** a speciality of the region?

> **What do you recommend** as a starter?
> **What do you recommend** for dessert?
> You've been to this restaurant before, Pilar. **What do you recommend?**

To give you an idea about what to eat, you might ask someone at your table what they have chosen. Use **What are you having ... ?**.

> **What are you having**, Juan?
> **What are you having** for dessert, Yuta?
> **What are you having** for your starter?

If you want to ask whether you should have or do something, use **Do you think I should ... ?**.

> **Do you think I should** have the tart?
> **Do you think I should** try the snails?
> **Do you think we should** leave a tip?

Useful words

local	in or relating to the area where you live
a speciality	a special food or product that is always very good in a particular place
a region	an area of the country or of the world
a tart	a case made of flour, fat and water (=pastry) that you fill with fruit or vegetables and cook in an oven
a snail	a small animal with a long, soft body, no legs and a shell on its back
a tip	money that you give to someone to thank them for a job that they have done for you

Making suggestions

The simplest way to make a suggestion is to use **We could ...** .

> **We could** eat here, if you like.
> **We could** just have a salad.

If you want to make a suggestion and see if other people agree with you, use **Shall we ... ?**.

> **Shall we** order?
> **Shall we** see what that new French restaurant is like?

If you have an idea about something, use **How about ... ?**.

> **How about** finding somewhere to eat in town?
> **How about** sharing a dessert?

Another way to make a suggestion is to say **Why don't ... ?**.

> **Why don't** we ask Neel to join us?
> **Why don't** you walk to the restaurant and taxi home?

I suggest ... is a slightly stronger way of making a suggestion.

> **I suggest** you get a taxi to the restaurant.
> **I suggest** we order a variety of dishes and then share them.

> **GOOD TO KNOW!**
> After **I suggest**, the verb that follows 'I/you/we, etc.' is the normal present tense. It should not have 'to' before it.

Useful words

share	to have or use something with another person
taxi	to travel by taxi
a variety	a number of things that are different from each other

Talking about your plans

To say what you have decided to eat, use **I'm having the ...** or **I'm going to have the ...** .

> **I'm having the** pie.
> **I'm having the** soup for a starter.

> **I'm going to have the** fish stew.
> **I'm going to have the** pasta for my main course.

If you do not know what to choose, use **I can't decide what to have ...** .

> **I can't decide what to have** for a starter.
> **I can't decide what to have** for a main course.
> There are so many delicious things. **I can't decide what to have**.

If you think you might choose something, use **Perhaps I'll have the ...** .

> **Perhaps I'll have the** salad for my starter.
> **Perhaps I'll have the** salmon for my main course.

If you change your decision about what you are going to eat, use **I've changed my mind ...** .

> **I've changed my mind** – I'm having the lamb for a starter.
> **I've changed my mind** – I'm not having a dessert.
> **She's changed her mind** – she's going to have the soup for a starter.

Useful words

a pie	a dish of fruit, meat or vegetables that is covered with pastry (= a mixture of flour, butter and water) and baked
a stew	a meal that you make by cooking meat and vegetables in water
delicious	very good to eat
salmon	the pink flesh of a large silver fish that people eat

● Listen out for

Here are some useful phrases you may hear in a restaurant.

Do you have a reservation?
I'm sorry, we're full.
This way please.
Follow me please.
Smoking or non-smoking?
Here's the menu.
Would you like to see the dessert menu?
Can I take your order?
And for you, Sir?
And for you, Madam?
Today's specials are on the board.
I'd recommend the *tarte tatin*.
Are you ready to order?
The pasta comes with a green salad.
Would you like a drink first?
What will you have to drink?
Can I get you something to drink?
Would you like anything else?
Can I get you anything else?
Is that everything?
Is everything all right?
I'll be right with you.
I'll bring it right away.

Useful words

a reservation	a room or a seat that a hotel, a transport company or a restaurant keeps ready for you
full	containing as many people as possible
a special	a dish in a restaurant that is only available on a particular day and is not usually available
right away	immediately

Listen to the conversation: Track 7

Emma and her friend Ashley are making arrangements to go out to dinner.

A I'd quite like to try that new Swedish restaurant next to Walkers on Main Street.

B Me too. Let's go there.

A Great. Shall we invite Miyoko? I haven't seen her for ages.

B Yeah, good idea – I'd love to see her.

A Could you call her? I don't have her number.

B Sure. Should I book a table too?

A Yeah, we probably should – it's quite popular.

B What time should we meet then?

A How does seven o'clock sound?

B Would you mind if we met a little later – seven-thirty, say? I don't leave work till six o'clock on a Thursday and I might struggle to get there for seven.

A Yes, of course. That's absolutely fine.

B How are you getting there, by the way?

A I thought I'd walk, though it's quite a long way from here.

B Would you prefer it if I drove you there? I could pick you up at around seven o'clock, if you like?

A That would be great. We could park nearby on Cotswold Lane – there are usually spaces there.

B Perfect. See you at seven o'clock tonight, hopefully with Miyoko.

A See you then!

 Listen to more phrases and practise saying them: Track 8

Going out

Have a good time!

If you are going out, whether it is to a party, a concert or the cinema, these phrases will help you say what you want, ask where things are and ask for what you need.

Making suggestions

One easy way of making a suggestion about where you and a friend can go and what you can do, is to use **We could ...** .

> **We could** go and see a film.
> **We could** go to a nightclub, if you like.
> **We could** go to the theatre, if you like.

> **GOOD TO KNOW!**
> When people start a sentence with **We could ...** they often add **if you like** at the end.

If you are eager to do something with someone, use **Let's ...** .

> **Let's** go to the cinema.
> **Let's** buy tickets for Saturday's match.
> I've got a good idea. **Let's** all go swimming.

Another way to make a suggestion about where to go and what to do is to use **Shall we ... ?**.

> **Shall we** go out for dinner?
> **Shall we** have a barbecue and invite some friends round?
> **Shall we** all go out for a walk?

Useful words

a nightclub	a place where people go late in the evening to dance
a match	a sports game between two people or teams
a barbecue	a party where you cook food on a piece of equipment outdoors

If you have an idea about what to do or where to go, use **How about ... ?** or **What about ... ?**.

> **How about** going somewhere for a coffee?
> **How about** going bowling?

> **What about** going somewhere where we can dance?
> **What about** taking a picnic to the park?

> **GOOD TO KNOW!**
> **How about/What about + -ing**
> A verb that comes after **How about ... ?** or **What about ... ?** must be in the -ing form.

To suggest what someone else can do or where someone else can go, use **You could ...** .

> **You could** go to a concert.
> After your meal, **you could** have ice-creams on the terrace.

You can also use **Why not ... ?** or **Why don't ... ?** if you have an idea about what someone else might do.

> **Why not** invite some friends from work?
> If you don't have anything to do, **why not** go to Helena's party?

> **Why don't** we have a party for him?
> **Why don't** you come along to the party after the film?

Useful words

bowling	a game in which you roll a heavy ball down a narrow track toward a group of wooden objects and try to knock down as many of them as possible
a picnic	when you eat a meal outdoors, usually in a park or a forest, or at the beach
a concert	a performance of music
a terrace	a flat area next to a building where people can sit

I suggest ... and **You should ...** are slightly strong ways of making a suggestion.

> **I suggest** we get a taxi there.
> **You should** invite her husband too.

Talking about your plans

The simplest way of talking about a plan that you are sure of is to use **I'm** followed by a verb in the **-ing** form.

> **I'm seeing** Julio and Sasha tonight.
> **We're having** a party for Pia on Saturday.

The simplest way of asking someone what they plan to do is **What are you doing ... ?**.

> **What are you doing** tonight?
> **What are you doing** for your birthday?

For a plan that you are sure of, you can also use **I'm going to ...** . Use **Are you going to ... ?** to ask someone if they will do something.

> **I'm going to** go out with some friends tonight.
> **We're going to** have dinner at our friends' house tonight.

> **Are you going to** celebrate now that you've finished your exams?
> **Are you going to** invite many people to the party?

Useful words

go out	to leave your home to do something enjoyable
celebrate	to do something enjoyable for a special reason

You can use **I'm planning to ...** or **I plan to ...**, for something that you want to do, but which is not certain.

> **I'm planning to** invite my neighbours.
> **We're planning to** call in on our way home.

> **I plan to** take her out for dinner while I'm in New York.
> **I plan to** have some friends over for my birthday.

To talk about something that you would like to do but are not sure that you will do, you can use **I'm hoping to ...** or **I hope to ...** .

> **I'm hoping to** see them in concert.
> **He's hoping to** see some theatre while he's there.

> **I hope to** have dinner with Gunilla while I'm in Sweden.
> **We hope to** go to the ballet while we're in Moscow.

To talk about a plan that is only possible, use **I might ...** .

> **I might** see a band at the weekend.
> **I might** meet up with Farida and Saki tonight.
> **We might** go to a club afterwards.

To talk about what should happen in the future, use **I'm supposed to ...** .

> **I'm supposed to** be at the restaurant at eight o'clock.
> **I'm supposed to** be home in half an hour.

Useful words

a neighbour	someone who lives near you
call in	to visit someone
take someone out	to take someone somewhere enjoyable
ballet	a type of dancing with carefully planned movements
a band	a group of people who play music together
meet up	to come together with people

Asking for information

Use **Is ... ?** to ask general questions requiring information.

> **Is** the club generally busy on a Friday night?
> **Is** the club open to under 21-year-olds?
> **Is** it expensive to go to the ballet?

Use **Is there ... ?** or **Do you have ... ?** to ask whether something exists.

> Excuse me, **is there** a cinema in this part of town?
> **Is there** a football match on this afternoon?
> Excuse me, **are there** any free concerts on this weekend?

> **Do you have** any tickets left?
> **Do you have** any tickets for tonight's performance?
> **Do you have** any programmes?

If you want to know the time that something happens, use **What time ... ?**.

> **What time** does the film start?
> **What time** does the concert finish?
> **What time** shall we meet?

To ask how much time something lasts for, use **How long ... ?**.

> **How long** is the film?
> **How long** is the concert?
> **How long** will you be in this café?

Useful words	
busy	full of people who are doing things
left	still there after everything else has gone or been used
a performance	when you entertain an audience by singing, dancing or acting
a programme	a small book or sheet of paper that tells you about a play or concert

If you want to ask about the money that you need to do something, use **How much ... ?**.

> **How much** is it to get in?
> **How much** is a theatre ticket?
> **How much** does it cost to watch the match?

To ask how to do something, use **How do you ... ?**.

> **How do you** get tickets for a match?
> **How do you** find out a good place to eat?
> **How do you** get to the town centre?

Asking for things

To ask for something, use **Can I have ... ?** or **Could I have ... ?**. To be polite, use please at the beginning or end of the question.

> **Can I have** two tickets for the show, please?
> **Can I have** a concert programme, please?

> **Could I have** a cola, please?
> **Could I have** a taxi for 7 Malvern Street?

Another way of asking for something is **I'd like ...** .

> **I'd like** an orange juice, please.
> **I'd like** a ticket for the Rouen-Cherbourg match.
> **I'd like** three tickets, please.

Useful words

a show	a performance in a theatre
cola	a sweet brown drink with bubbles in it
juice	the liquid from a fruit or a vegetable

If you are asking someone if they can do something for you, use **Can you ... ?** or **Could you ... ?**. **Could you ... ?** is slightly more polite and formal than **Can you... ?**. To be polite, use **please** at the beginning or end of these sentences.

> **Can you** tell me where the toilets are, please?
> **Can you** find a seat while I go to the toilets?

> **Could you** take me to Jewels nightclub, please.
> **Could you** get me a drink, please?

Saying what you like, dislike, prefer

To talk about things you like, use **I like ...** and to ask someone if they like something, use **Do you like ... ?**.

> **I like** going to see bands play.
> **I like** going out with my friends.
> **He likes** dance music.

> **Do you like** dancing?
> **Do you like** horror films?
> **Do you like** eating out?

> **GOOD TO KNOW!**
> **like + -ing**
> When **like ...** is followed by a verb, the verb is usually in the -ing form.

If you like something, but not in a strong way, use **I quite like ...** .

> **I quite like** going to the cinema.
> **I quite like** the theatre.
> **I quite like** going out in the evenings but usually I prefer to stay in.

Useful words

a horror film	a film that is intended to frighten you
eat out	to eat in a restaurant
stay in	to remain at home and not go out

going out 71

If you like something very much, you can say **I really like ...** or **I love ...** .

> **I really like** having picnics in the park in the summer.
> **I really like** going to the opera.
> **I really like** live music.

> **I love** having dinner with my friends.
> **I love** taking taxis.
> I absolutely **love** musicals.

To tell someone what you do not like, use **I don't like ...** .

> **I don't like** football.
> **I don't like** going to the theatre.
> **I don't** really **like** science fiction films.

A slightly formal way of saying what you don't like is **I dislike ...** .

> **I dislike** having to queue to get in.
> **I dislike** paying restaurant prices.
> **He dislikes** noisy places.

To say very strongly that you do not like something, use **I hate ...** .

> **I hate** opera.
> **I hate** being in a crowd.
> I absolutely **hate** noisy clubs.

Useful words

opera	a play with music in which all the words are sung
live music	music that is performed before an audience
a musical	a play or a film that uses singing or dancing in the story
science fiction	stories in books, magazines and films about things that happen in the future or in other parts of the universe
queue	to join a line of people or vehicles that are waiting for something
noisy	making a lot of loud or unpleasant noise
a crowd	a large group of people who have gathered together

> **GOOD TO KNOW!**
> **Hate + -ing**
> When **hate ...** is followed by a verb, the verb is usually in the -ing form.

If you want to say that you like one thing more than another, use **I prefer ...** .
If you want to talk about the thing you like less, use **to** before it.

> He doesn't really like socializing. **He prefers** to stay in and read a good book.
> **I prefer** going to the cinema **to** watching DVDs at home.
> **I prefer** having dinner at friends' houses **to** eating in restaurants.

Expressing opinions

Use **I thought ...** to give your opinion of a film you have seen, a concert you have been to or something else that you have done.

> **I thought** it was a really good film.
> **I thought** the play was a bit long.
> **I thought** it was an excellent concert.

If you want to ask other people if they think something is good or bad, use **What did you think of ... ?**.

> **What did you think of** the band?
> **What did you think of** her voice?
> **What did you think of** the meal?

Useful words

socialize	to meet other people socially, for example at parties
excellent	extremely good
your voice	the sound that comes out from your mouth when you speak or sing

You can also ask someone for their opinion by saying **What's your opinion of ... ?**.

> **What's your opinion of** her latest film?
> **What's your opinion of** the new club that has just opened on Kings Lane?

To agree with someone's opinion, use **I agree**. If you want to say who you agree with, use **with**.

> 'This is a really cool nightclub.' 'I agree'.
> **I agree with** Francine. It's a fantastic restaurant.
> I completely **agree with** you. It was a terrible match.

You can also use **You're right ...** to agree with what someone has said.

> **'You're right** – she can't sing!'
> I think **you're right**. His last film was much better.
> Luca**'s right**. The food here is great.

If you do not agree with someone, you can use **I don't agree.** This is quite strong, so to be more polite, you might say **I'm afraid I don't agree.** or **I don't really agree.** You could also use **I disagree ...** . If you want to say who you disagree with, use **with**.

> 'It's a great venue.' '**I don't really agree**. I think it's too small for this
>   number of people.'
> 'Anyway, Carla seemed happy enough with her party.' '**I don't agree**.
>   I thought she seemed a bit disappointed.'
> 'It was such a dull film.' '**I don't agree with** you. I thought it was great.'

Useful words

cool	fashionable and interesting
a nightclub	a place where people go late in the evening to drink and dance
fantastic	very good
a venue	the place where an event or an activity happens
disappointed	sad because something has not happened or because something is not as good as you hoped
dull	boring

'I think the nightlife in the city has really improved.' 'I'm afraid **I disagree**.' I'm afraid **I disagree with** you there.

I disagree with Martine. There's very little for young people to do in the evening in this village.

You can also use **I don't think ...** to disagree with someone.

'That restaurant has really improved.' '**I don't think** it has. I had a really bad meal there a month ago.'

'It's the best club in town.' '**I don't think** so. I much prefer Dino's.'

'It was a good show but it was too long.' 'Did you think so? **I didn't think** it was.'

Asking for permission

If you need to ask if you can do something when you are out, the simplest way is to use **Can I ... ?**.

Can I pay by card?

Can we sit outside?

A more formal way of asking for permission is to use **May I ... ?**.

May I take this chair?

May I sit anywhere?

If you want to make sure that someone will not be unhappy or angry if you do something, use **Do you mind if ... ?**.

Do you mind if I get to the restaurant a bit later?

Do you mind if I join you?

Do you mind if we sit here?

Useful words

nightlife	entertainment at night, for example nightclubs
a bit	a little
join	to come together with other people

You can also use **Is it OK ... ?**. This is slightly informal, but you can use it in most situations.

> **Is it OK** to take my mobile in with me?
> **Is it OK** to leave my bag here?
> **Is it OK** to eat inside the cinema?

To ask if something is allowed, use **Are we allowed to ... ?**.

> **Are we allowed to** take pictures?
> **Are we allowed to** speak during the performance?

● **Listen out for**

Here are some important phrases that are connected with going out.

Are you free tomorrow night?
What are you doing tonight?
Would you like to go out?
How about next week?
When would be a good time for you?
I'm afraid I'm busy.
I'm busy next week.
I'd love to.
Maybe another time.

Where would you like to sit?
Smoking or non-smoking?
Can I see your tickets, please?
Would you like to buy a programme?

Let me get you a drink.
What can I get you?
Did you have a good time tonight?
Thank you for inviting me.
It was a great party.
We really enjoyed the party.

Useful words

free	not doing anything else and so able to do something
busy	already doing something, so that you are not free to do something else

Listen to the conversation: Track 9

Emma and Ashley are deciding how to celebrate Ashley's birthday.

A So what are you doing for your birthday? Have you decided?

B I'm not sure. I might just have a few friends around to my house in the evening.

A If the weather's nice you could have a barbecue.

B That's a good idea. I love having people round in the summer when everyone can eat in the garden.

A I could help you with it, if you like.

B That would be great – thanks! I'd probably need a bit of help as I'm hoping to see my parents during the day. They're in the UK for a couple of weeks, and they're coming over to Oxford to take me out for lunch.

A How lovely!

B Yes, it should be nice. It means I won't get back till early evening so if you could help me prepare the food, that would be great.

A I have an idea. Why don't you ask everyone to bring a dish? That should make things simpler.

B Oh yes! That's a great idea.

A What shall I bring?

B How about that delicious salad you made for Davina's party?

A Oh yes, sure. I'll do a dessert too. What about a chocolate cake?

B Lovely! I'd better start inviting people. I'm seeing Gabriella and Artur tonight so I'll start by asking them.

 Listen to more phrases and practise saying them: Track 10

Days out

Have a nice day!

If you are planning to see the sights in a city or country, these phrases will help you to ask where you can go, what you can do there and how much it will cost.

Saying what you want to do

The simplest way of saying what you want to do is to use **I'd like to ...** .

> **I'd like to** go to the aquarium.
> **We'd like to** go up the church tower.

If you are very eager to do something, use **I'd really like to ...** or **I'd love to ...** .

> **I'd really like to** see the Great Wall of China.
> **I'd really like to** take some photos of the town.

> **I'd love to** go walking in the mountains.
> **I'd love to** visit the palace.

Use **I'd rather ...** when you want to do one thing and not another. If you want to mention the thing that you do not want, you should use **than** before it.

> **I'd rather** go to the beach **than** see an art exhibition.
> **We'd rather** take a boat trip **than** go walking.
> **I'd rather** visit some of the ancient Roman ruins.

Useful words	
an aquarium	a building where fish and sea animals are kept
a tower	a tall, narrow building, or a tall part of another building
a palace	a very large and impressive house where a king, a queen or a president lives
an exhibition	a public event where art or interesting objects are shown
ancient	very old, or from a long time ago
ruins	the parts of a building that remain after something destroys the rest

Talking about your plans

We often use **I'm + -ing verb** or **I'm going to ...** to talk about plans for a day out.

> **I'm going** to the Tower of London tomorrow.
> **We're taking** my parents to the theatre.
> **She's seeing** the Monet exhibition this afternoon.

> **I'm going to** phone to check that the museum's open on Mondays.
> **He's going to** hire a guide for the day.
> **We're going to** take the kids with us.

Use **Are you going to ... ?** or **Will you ... ?** to ask someone about their plans.

> **Are you going to** buy a guidebook?
> **Are you going to** visit the Acropolis?

> **Will you** spend all day at the museum?
> **Will you** have time to see the gardens?

You can also use **I'm planning to ...** or **I'm hoping to ...** to say what you intend to do. **I'm hoping to ...** is slightly less definite.

> **I'm planning to** visit the Niagara Falls while I'm in Canada.
> **She's planning to** spend the day at the botanic gardens.
> **We're planning to** take a picnic to the beach.

Useful words

hire	to pay someone to do a job for you
a guide	someone who shows tourists around places such as museums or cities
a guidebook	a book for tourists that gives information about a town, an area or a country
botanic gardens	a place with interesting plants, trees and grass that people can visit
a picnic	a meal that you eat outdoors

I'm hoping to be able to see the rock paintings.
I'm hoping to go on a walk in the rainforest.
We're hoping to see some dolphins.

I intend to ... is a rather strong and definite way of talking about your plans.

I intend to take some photographs of the Taj Mahal.
I intend to walk all the way around the city walls.
I intend to climb all three mountains in a day.

To talk about what should happen in the future, use **I'm supposed to ...** .

I'm supposed to be bringing a picnic.
What time **are we supposed to** get there?
He's supposed to be meeting me this morning.

Making suggestions

The simplest way to make a suggestion is to use **You could ...** .

You could go on a guided tour of the city.
We could ask Janne to show us the old town.

To make a suggestion about something you think would be good to do with other people, use **Shall we ... ?**.

Shall we go to the beach?
Shall we try and climb to the top?

Useful words

a rainforest	a thick forest with tall trees that grows in tropical areas where there is a lot of rain
a dolphin	a large grey or black and white intelligent animal that lives in the sea
a guided tour	a trip around an interesting place with someone who tells you about it

Use **How about ... ?** if you have an idea about what to do.

> **How about** taking a boat trip round the harbour?
> **How about** going to the Picasso museum?

> **GOOD TO KNOW!**
> **How about + -ing**
> The verb that comes after **How about ... ?** must be in the -ing form.

Another way to make a suggestion is to say **Why don't ... ?** .

> **Why don't** we see if the castle is open to the public?
> **Why don't** we go for a walk in the forest?
> **Why don't** you take her to the carnival?

I suggest ... and **We should ...** are slightly strong ways of making a suggestion.

> **I suggest** we go to the visitor centre first.
> **I suggest** you take a map with you.
> **I suggest** she meets us in the park.

> **GOOD TO KNOW!**
> After **I suggest**, the verb that follows 'I/you/we, etc.' is the normal present tense. It should not have 'to' before it.

> **We should** visit the Louvre before we leave Paris.
> **We should** take some photos of Chinatown.
> **They should** go to the motor museum.

Useful words
a harbour — an area of water next to the land where boats can safely stay
a carnival — a celebration in the street, with music and dancing
a visitor centre — a building where you can get information about a place

Asking for information

Use **Is ... ?** to ask general questions about things.

> **Is** the castle interesting?
> **Is** the museum free or do you have to pay?
> **Is** it far to the ice rink?

Use **Is there ... ?** or **Do you have ... ?** to ask whether something exists.

> Excuse me, **is there** a tourist information office near here?
> **Is there** anywhere to leave our coats?
> **Are there** any cheaper tickets?

> **Do you have** disabled access?
> **Do you have** any activities for children?
> **Do you have** a restaurant?

To ask about the time, use **What time ... ?** .

> **What time** does the park close?
> **What time** is the next guided tour?
> **What time** do we get there?

To ask about the time that something will take, use **How long ... ?** .

> **How long** does the tour last?
> **How long** is the boat trip?
> **How long** does it take to get there?

Useful words

an ice rink	a place where people go to skate (= move over ice on special shoes)
a tourist	a person who is visiting a place on holiday
disabled	having an injury or an illness that makes it difficult for you to do some things
access	when you are able to go into a particular place

To ask how to do something, use **How do you ... ?** .

> **How do you** get to the old town?
> **How do you** book tickets?
> **How do you** reserve a seat?

> **GOOD TO KNOW!**
> **How do you + infinitive**
> The verb that comes after **How do you ... ?** must be in the infinitive without 'to'.

Asking for things

To ask for something, use **Can I have ... ?**, **Could I have ... ?** or **I'd like ...** .
To be polite, use **please** at the beginning or end.

> **Can I have** two tickets for tonight's performance, please?
> **Can I have** an audio guide, please?

> **Could I have** a programme for this evening's concert?
> **Could we have** three seats together?

> **I'd like** a map of the area, please.
> **I'd like** front-row seats, if possible.

Useful words

book	to arrange to have or use something, such as a hotel room or a ticket to a concert, at a later time
reserve	to keep something for a particular person or purpose
a performance	when you entertain an audience by singing, dancing or acting
an audio guide	a piece of equipment that gives you spoken information about a place
a programme	a small book or piece of paper that tells you about a play or concert
front-row	in the line of seats at the front of a theatre

If it is important for you to have something, you can use **I need ...** .

> **I need** the address of the museum.
> **I need** a street map of the city.
> **We need** a guide who can speak English.

If you want to ask if something you want is available, use **Do you have ... ?** or **Do you do ... ?** .

> **Do you have** any brochures in English?
> **Do you have** any information on trips in this area?
> **Do you have** any tickets left for tomorrow's show?

> **Do you do** discounts for students?
> **Do you do** guided tours?
> **Do you do** tours in other languages?

If you are asking someone if they can do something for you, the simplest way is to use **Can you ... ?** or **Could you ... ?** . **Could you ... ?** is slightly more polite and formal than **Can you ... ?** .

> **Can you** tell me what the opening hours are?
> Please **can you** show me where we are on this map?

> **Could you** check if I've got the right tickets?
> **Could you** tell me the way to the theatre?

Useful words

a brochure	a thin magazine with pictures that gives you information about a place, a product or a service
a discount	a reduction in the usual price of something
opening hours	the times that a place is open

A polite way of asking someone to do something is by saying **Would you mind ... ?** .

>**Would you mind** showing me where the Egyptian exhibits are kept?
>**Would you mind** checking that I've got the right tickets?
>**Would you mind** translating this into English?

To ask whether something you want is possible, use **Is it possible ... ?** .

>**Is it possible** to change these tickets for a later performance?
>**Is it possible** to get cheaper tickets nearer the time?
>**Is it possible** to hire a German-speaking guide?

Asking for permission

If you need to ask if you can do something, the most simple way is to use **Can I ... ?**.

>**Can I** use this ticket on the bus as well?
>**Can we** park our car here?

A more formal way of asking for permission is to use **May I ... ?** .

>**May I** borrow this guidebook?
>**May we** look around the gardens?
>**May we** see the room where he worked?

If you want to check that someone will not be unhappy or angry if you do something, use **Do you mind if ... ?** .

>**Do you mind if** we turn up a bit late?
>**Do you mind if** he brings a friend?
>**Do you mind if** I leave the pushchair here?

Useful words

an exhibit	an object such as a painting that is shown to the public
translate	to say or write something again in a different language
turn up	to arrive
a pushchair	a small chair on wheels used for moving a young child around

You can also use **Is it OK ... ?**. This is slightly informal, but you can use it in most situations.

> **Is it OK** to take photos?
> **Is it OK** to use this entrance?
> **Is it OK** if I record your talk?

To ask if something is allowed, use **Are we allowed to ... ?** .

> **Are we allowed to** take drinks into the cinema?
> **Are we allowed to** come back in again later?
> **Are we allowed to** use these tickets on the river boat?

Saying what you like, dislike, prefer

The simplest way to talk about things you like is to use **I like ...** . To talk about activities that you like doing, use **I enjoy ...** .

> **I like** visiting modern art galleries.
> **I like** this sculpture very much.
> **Do you like** going to concerts?

> **I enjoy** going on guided tours.
> **I really enjoy** learning about history.
> **Do you enjoy** going to the ballet?

Useful words

the entrance	the door or gate where you go into a place
record	to store sounds so that they can be heard again
a gallery	a place where people go to look at art
a sculpture	a piece of art that is made into a shape from a material like stone or wood
ballet	a type of dancing with carefully planned movements

> **GOOD TO KNOW!**
> **Like/Enjoy + -ing**
> When **like ...** or **enjoy ...** is followed by a verb, the verb is usually in the -ing form.

If you like something very much, you can say **I love ...** .

> **I love** the small villages of Provence.
> **I love** this type of architecture.
> **I love** going to art galleries.

To tell someone what you do not like, use **I don't like ...** , or to make your view stronger, **I hate ...** .

> **I don't like** bus tours.
> **I don't like** roller-coasters.
> **I don't like** Shakespeare.

> **I hate** being late.
> I really **hate** horror movies.
> **I hate** travelling by underground.

A slightly formal way of saying what you don't like is **I dislike ...** .

> **I dislike** having to queue.
> **She dislikes** using public transport.

> **GOOD TO KNOW!**
> **Hate/Dislike + -ing**
> When **hate ...** or **dislike ...** is followed by a verb, the verb is usually in the -ing form.

Useful words

architecture	the style of the design of a building
a roller-coaster	a thing like a fast train that goes up and down very steep slopes as an exciting entertainment
a horror movie	a very frightening film
queue	to stand in a line of people that are waiting for something
public transport	a system of vehicles such as buses and trains that the public use

If you want to say that you like one thing more than another, use **I prefer ...** .
If you want to talk about the thing you like less, use **to** before it.

>**I prefer** museums **to** religious buildings.
>**She prefers** walking **to** cycling.
>**I prefer** to avoid that area.

To say that you would prefer to do something, use **I'd rather ...** . If you want to
talk about the thing you like less, use **than**.

>**I'd rather** do something outdoors **than** go to a museum.
>**I'd rather** spend the whole week in Marseilles.
>**We'd rather** walk **than** take the bus.

To talk about something that you would prefer not to do, use **I'd prefer not to
...** or **I'd rather not ...** .

>**I'd prefer not to** travel by boat.
>**We'd prefer not to** have to carry our own luggage.

>**I'd rather not** stay much longer.
>**I'd rather not** go on the roller-coaster.

>**GOOD TO KNOW!**
>Remember **that I'd rather not ...** does not have 'to' before the infinitive.

Useful words
avoid   to keep away from a person, place or thing
outdoors   happening outside rather than in a building

Complaining

You may have to complain about something which you're unhappy with. You could start your complaint with **I'm not happy ...** or **I'm disappointed ...** .

> **I'm not happy** with our guide.
> **I'm not happy** about having to pay extra for the children.
> **I wasn't happy** that the pool was closed.

> **I'm disappointed** with the way we were treated.
> **She was disappointed** about not seeing any lions.
> The children **were disappointed** that they didn't get to see the clowns.

You can use **I think ...** to give your opinion about what is wrong with a place or an event.

> **I think** it's a bit expensive for what it is.
> **I think** that they need to clean the toilets more often.
> **I don't think** it's very well organized.
> **I didn't think** the museum was very interesting.
> **I thought** the speakers were badly prepared.

Useful words

a clown   a performer who wears funny clothes and does silly things to make people laugh

● Listen out for

Here are some useful phrases you may hear on your day out.

> Press here to select the language you want.
> Here's a leaflet in English.
> Do you have a student card?
> The museum's open from nine to three.
> The gallery's closed on Sundays.
> The next guided tour's at ten.
> It's eight euros each.
> You're not allowed to take pictures.
> Can I search your bag?
> Please leave your bag and coat in the cloakroom.
> Please make a donation to support our museum.
> Please supervise your children at all times.

Useful words	
select	to choose one particular person or thing from a group of similar people or things
a leaflet	a piece of paper containing information about a particular subject
a cloakroom	a room in a building where you can leave your coat
a donation	money that is given to help an organization
supervise	to make sure that someone behaves well or does something correctly

Brett and Emma have decided to spend the day together on Saturday.
They're talking about what to do.

A What shall we do on Saturday, Emma? I was hoping to see the Monet exhibition some time – do you fancy that?

B The weather's so nice at the moment, I'd rather do something outside, if you don't mind. How about going to the park?

A That would be great. What shall we do about lunch? Do they have a café there?

B They do, but it's not very nice. I suggest we buy some sandwiches on the way and take them in with us.

A Good idea. I'm planning to meet Nuria at six, so we'll have to be back by five at the latest.

B That's fine.

Brett has arrived at the Museum of Archaeology and is talking to a member of staff.

A I'm hoping to see the Roman exhibiton. Do you have any information about it?

B We have this brochure.

A How much is it?

B It's 5 pounds.

A I'll have one, please.

B OK, that's 5 pounds then. Would you like to leave your bag in the cloakroom?

A I'd prefer not to – I've got some expensive camera equipment in there. By the way, is it OK to take photos inside the museum?

B No, I'm sorry, we don't allow photographs.

A That's a shame. I'm supposed to be giving a talk to my history club, and I wanted to show some pictures.

 Listen to more phrases and practise saying them: Track 12

Shopping

Can I help you?

Whether you're planning to shop for clothes or things for your home, buy food or just pick up a postcard, this unit will give you all the phrases you need to do your shopping.

Asking for things

The simplest way to ask for something in a shop is to use **I'd like ...** or **Could I have ... ?** .

> **I'd like** two kilos of potatoes, please.
> **I'd like** a case for my camera.
> **I'd like** a melon that's nice and ripe, please.

> **Could I have** a packet of envelopes, please?
> **Could I have** a 10 litre pot of white paint?
> **Could I have** a carrier bag, please?

You can also say what you are looking for by using **I'm looking for ...** .

> **I'm looking for** vegetable seeds.
> **I'm looking for** brown rice.

A slightly informal way of saying what you want is **I'm after ...** .

> **I'm after** a good quality garden table.
> **I'm after** some really juicy apples.

Useful words

a melon	a large fruit with soft, sweet flesh and hard green or yellow skin
ripe	used for describing fruit or vegetables that are ready to eat
an envelope	the paper cover in which you put a letter before you send it to someone
a carrier bag	a plastic or paper bag with handles that you use for carrying shopping
juicy	containing a lot of juice
a bulb	the glass part inside a lamp that gives out light
a torch	a small electric light that you carry in your hand

To ask if a shop sells the thing you want, use **Do you sell ... ?** or **Have you got ... ?** .

> **Do you sell** light bulbs?
> **Do you sell** printer paper?
> **Do you sell** plant pots?

> **Have you got** any white shirts?
> **Have you got** a battery that will fit my hearing aid?
> **Have you got** the right colour polish for these shoes?

In a shop where an assistant fetches things, you could say **Can you give me ... , please?** .

> **Can you give me** five of those oranges, **please?**
> **Can you give me** ten first-class stamps, **please?**
> **Can you give me** three metres of this cloth, **please?**

When you have decided what you want to buy, use **I'll have ...** or **I'll take ...** .

> **I'll take** the handbag.
> **I'll take** the big saucepan.
> **I'll take** two of those pineapples.

> **I'll have** some bananas.
> **I'll have** a wholemeal loaf.
> **I'll have** three dozen red roses.

Useful words

a hearing aid	a small piece of equipment that people wear in their ear to help them to hear better
polish	a substance that you put on shoes in order to clean them and make them shine
wholemeal	made using whole grains
a dozen	twelve

Saying what you have to do

If you need to buy something, use **I have to ...** or **I've got to ...** .

> **I have to** buy Richard a birthday card.
> **I have to** stop at the baker's.
> **You have to** ask the shop assistant if you want to try things on.
> **We have to** buy a new vacuum cleaner.

> **I've got to** get a memory stick for my college work.
> **I've got to** order the books in time for the course.
> **I've got to** buy some food for tonight.

You could also use **I need to ...** .

> **I need to** get something to wear to Flora's wedding.
> **I need to** make sure I get receipts for everything.
> **I need to** take back that dress I bought.

To talk about some shopping that is very important, use **I must ...** .

> **I must** find a birthday present for my sister.
> **I must** buy a suit for the interview.
> **I must** get a new briefcase.

Useful words

a vacuum cleaner and dirt	an electric machine that cleans surfaces by sucking up dust
a memory stick	a small electronic device for storing computer information
order	to ask for something to be sent to you from a company
a receipt	a piece of paper that shows that you have paid for something
a briefcase	a small suitcase for carrying business papers in

Use **I ought to ...** to talk about things you feel you should do.

> **I ought to** buy some low-energy light bulbs.
> **I ought to** shop locally more often.
> **I ought to** try that baker's Fiona recommended.

Talking about your plans

To tell someone what you are going to do, use **I'm going to ...** or **I'll ...** .

> **I'm going to** buy a new carpet.
> **I'm going to** wait for the sales and see if I can get it cheaper.
> **We're going to** go to the new shopping centre.
> **Are you going to** get a better TV?

> **I'll** get some flowers for Diana.
> **I'll** try to find a duvet cover that matches the curtains.
> **I'll** find out how much a new printer would cost.

To tell someone about a plan you have, use **I'm planning to ...** .

> **I'm planning to** buy a new outfit for the party.
> **I'm planning to** buy him a tennis racket for his birthday.
> **I'm planning to** spend the day shopping in London.

Useful words	
locally	in the area where you live
recommend	to suggest that someone would find a particular person or thing good or useful
the sales	a time when a shop sells things for less that their normal price
a duvet	a thick warm cover for a bed
match	to have the same colour or design as another thing, or to look good with it
an outfit	a set of clothes

You may want to talk about what you're thinking of buying or where you're thinking of going. Use **I'm thinking of...** .

> **I'm thinking of** going to the market tomorrow.
> **I'm thinking of** getting a laptop.
> **We're thinking of** buying a boat of our own.

For something you would like to do, but that is not certain, use **I'm hoping to ...** .

> **I'm hoping to** get some bargains.
> **I'm hoping to** find some boots to go with my dress.
> **We're hoping to** visit some antique shops.

Expressing opinions

When you look at things in shops, you may want to say what you think of them. Use **I think ...** .

> **I think** this material is beautiful.
> **I think** their cakes are the best in town.
> **I don't think** she'd like that bracelet.

You can also use **In my opinion ...** . This is quite a strong and slightly formal way of expressing your view.

> **In my opinion** the quality of their products has gone down.
> **In my opinion** this lipstick is slightly too dark.
> Where's the best place to buy a bike, **in your opinion**?

Useful words

an antique	an old object that is valuable because of its beauty or because of the way it was made
a bracelet	a piece of jewellery that you wear around your wrist
lipstick	a coloured substance that people sometimes put on their lips

To say things in a less strong way, use **I'd say ...** .

> **I'd say** it's a bit tight.
> **I'd say** that you need something warmer for winter.
> **I'd say** it's a bargain.

To agree with someone's else's opinion, use **I agree.** or **You're right.** .

> 'The assistants here are fantastic.' '**I agree**. They're always happy to give advice.'
> **I agree** with Helen that the leather chairs are more practical.
> 'The lighter jacket is more suitable for summer.' '**I agree.**'

> 'It's too tight around the waist.' '**You're right.** I need a bigger size.'
> **You're right** about this place – it's improved a lot since the new manager took over.
> 'It's not worth buying cheap clothes – they won't last.' '**You're right.** It's better to spend more and buy less.'

To disagree, you can say **I don't think so**. You can also say **I disagree** but this is quite strong.

> 'These linen trousers would be good for the journey.' '**I don't think so** – they crease too easily.
> 'Alla would love this shirt.' '**I don't** really **think so** – she prefers bright colours.'
> 'The assistants were so rude.' '**I didn't think so** – that young man was very helpful'

Useful words

tight	small, and fitting closely to your body
leather	animal skin that is used for making shoes, clothes, bags and furniture
practical	useful rather than being just fashionable or attractive
suitable	right for a particular purpose or occasion
your waist	the middle part of your body
take something over	to get control of something
linen	a type of strong cloth
crease	to form lines when pressed or folded
helpful	helping you by being useful or willing to work for you

'Buying organic food is a waste of money.' **I disagree**. It's good for you and good for the environment.

I disagree with what Naeem said about the butcher's.

'It's cheaper to buy larger quantities of food.' **I disagree** – if you do that, you end up throwing away a lot of it.

If you are shopping with someone else, you may want to ask for that person's opinion about something you are thinking of buying. Use **What do you think … ?** .

What do you think of these jeans?
What do you think of their furniture?
What do you think about buying a picnic rug?

Asking for information

For general information, use **Could you tell me … ?** .

Could you tell me if there's a bookshop here?
Could you tell me where I can get weedkiller?
Could you tell me the best place for children's clothes?

If you want to ask if a town has a particular shop, use **Is there … ?** .

Is there anywhere I can top up my phone?
Is there a florist in this town?
Is there a butcher's?

Useful words	
organic	grown without using chemicals
a butcher's	a shop where you can buy meat
a picnic rug	a piece of thick cloth that you put on the ground to sit on to eat outside
weedkiller	a substance that kills weeds (= plants that you do not want)
a florist	a shop where you can buy flowers

For asking where a shop is, or where something is in a shop, use **Where can I find ... ?**.

> **Where can I find** a hardware shop?
> **Where can I find** underwear?
> **Where can I find** the new Jacqueline Wilson book?

You can use **Is there ... ?** or **Do you have ... ?** to ask if a shop has something.

> **Is there** a changing room?
> **Is there** anyone who can explain the difference between these washing machines?
> **Is there** a gardening department?

> **Do you have** any dinner plates?
> **Do you have** it in a smaller size?
> **Do you have** any sunhats?

To ask for information about something you might buy, use **Is this ... ?** or **Is it ... ?** .

> **Is this** the best model?
> **Is this** available in any different colours?
> **Are these** in the sale?

> **Is it** genuine leather?
> **Is it** suitable for a child?
> **Are they** still in stock?

Useful words

hardware	tools and equipment that are used in the home and garden
underwear	clothes that you wear next to your skin, under your other clothes
a changing room	a room in a clothes shop where you can try clothes
a model	a particular design of something
genuine	true and real
in stock	available for you to buy

To ask a shop assistant for advice about what to buy, use **What would you recommend ... ?** .

> **What would you recommend** for painting iron railings?
> I'm looking for some garden furniture that will be OK in the rain.
> **What would you recommend?**
> **What would you recommend** for dry hair?

To ask for the price of something, use **How much is ... ?** .

> **How much is** the face cream?
> **How much are** the cherries per kilo?
> **How much are** your pineapples?

To ask whether you can do something, use **Can I ... ?** .

> **Can I** pay by credit card?
> **Can I** have it giftwrapped?
> **Can you** give me a discount, as it has a scratch on it?

Saying what you like, dislike, prefer

The simplest way to say what you like when you are shopping is **I like ...** .

> **I like** Italian cheese.
> **I like** this hat very much.
> Get it if **you like** it.
> **I don't like** the pattern.
> **I don't like** these gloves as much.

Useful words

a railing	a fence that is made from metal bars
per	for each
giftwrap	to put coloured paper around something so that it can be given as a present
a discount	a reduction in the usual price of something
a pattern	an arrangement of lines or shapes that form a design
a glove	a piece of clothing that you wear on your hand, with a separate part for each finger

If you have strong feelings about something, you could use **I love ...** or **I hate ...** .

> **I love** these chocolates.
> **I love** shopping with friends.
> **I love** trying on expensive clothes.

> **I hate** having to queue.
> **I hate** dresses like this.
> **I hate** aubergines.

> **GOOD TO KNOW!**
> **Like/Love/Hate + -ing**
> When **like**, **love** or **hate** are followed by a verb, the verb is usually in the -ing form.

To say that you like one thing more than another, use **I prefer ...** . If you want to talk about the thing you like less, use **to** before it.

> **I prefer** the one with the long sleeves.
> **We prefer** fresh produce **to** frozen.
> **I prefer** to buy things from independent shops.

To say what you would prefer to do, use **I'd rather ...** . If you want to talk about the thing you do not want to do, use **than** before it.

> **I'd rather** go for something more glamorous.
> **I'd rather** spend the money on CDs **than** books.
> **We'd rather** buy local produce.

Useful words	
queue	to stand in a line of people or vehicles waiting for something
an aubergine	a vegetable with a smooth, dark purple skin
a sleeve	one of the two parts of a piece of clothing that cover your arms
independent	not owned by a large company
glamorous	very attractive, exciting or interesting
local	in, or relating to, the area where you live
produce	food that you grow on a farm to sell

Making suggestions

If you are shopping with a friend, use **We could ...** to make suggestions.

> **We could** ask them to deliver it.
> **We could** see if they'll order one for us.
> **You could** ask them for a discount.

If you have an idea about something, use **How about ... ?** .

> **How about** going shopping this morning?
> **How about** trying that new bookshop?
> **How about** buying it online?

> **GOOD TO KNOW!**
> **How about + -ing**
> The verb that comes after **How about ... ?** must be in the -ing form.

You could also use **Why don't ... ?** or **Why not ... ?** .

> **Why don't** you wait for the sales?
> **Why don't** you treat yourself to a new suit?
> **Why don't** we look in another shop?

> **Why not** buy both shirts?
> **Why not** try it on?
> **Why not** ask David to pay for it?

> **GOOD TO KNOW!**
> **Why not + infinitive**
> The verb that comes after **Why not ... ?** must be in the infinitive without 'to'.

Useful words

deliver	to take something to a particular place

Asking for permission

To ask someone in a shop if you can do something, use **Can I ... ?** .

> **Can I** try on these sandals?
> **Can I** keep the hanger?
> **Can I** bring it back if I don't like it?
> **Can I** use this voucher to pay for it?
> **Can my daughter** try on this jacket?

A polite way of asking for permission is **Do you mind if I ... ?** .

> **Do you mind if I** try the other trousers on again?
> **Do you mind if I** take the wrapper off?
> **Do you mind if I** pay by credit card?

A slightly informal way of asking for permission is **Is it OK ... ?**.

> **Is it OK** if I have a closer look?
> **Is it OK** if I taste one of these cherries?
> **Is it OK** if I take the watch out of its box?

Useful words

a sandal	a light shoe that you wear in warm weather
a hanger	an object for hanging clothes on
a voucher	a piece of paper that can be used instead of money to pay for things
a wrapper	a piece of paper or plastic that covers something you buy

● Listen out for

Here are some useful phrases you may hear when out shopping.

Are you being served?
Can I help you?
How much were you thinking of spending?
We don't have any in stock just now.
We could order one for you, if you like.
We may have one in our other store.
Anything else?
Is it a present for someone?
Shall I giftwrap it for you?
Would you like to keep the hanger?
It's cash only, I'm afraid.
I'm afraid we don't take credit cards.
Could you sign here, please?
That comes to £34.57 altogether.
Can you put your PIN number in, please?
You can take your card now.
We don't do refunds on sale items.
Do you have your receipt?

Useful words
a refund   money that is returned to you because you have returned goods
to a shop

Listen to the conversation: Track 13

Brett has invited some friends for dinner. He goes to the Italian deli to buy food and to get some advice about what to cook.

A Hi. I'm cooking dinner for five people tomorrow evening. I need to get something that'll be quick so that I have time to prepare it after work.

B How about pasta? That's always popular, and we sell delicious fresh pasta.

A That sounds great. Can you give me enough for five people, please? And what would you recommend for the sauce?

B Why not try something spicy – maybe tomato with chilli, garlic and spicy sausage?

A I don't think my friend Ella would like that – she doesn't eat meat.

B Perhaps you could put in olives instead of the sausage? We have a great selection of olives.

A Oh, yes. Is it OK to try one or two?

B Sure.

A I'll take a large pot of the black ones. And I'm after something for dessert too. Do you have anything sweet?

Useful words

a deli   a shop that sells food such as cold meat and cheeses

B   We have things like panforte, which is made of sugar, fruit and nuts.
That's great with coffee. Or we have lots of great ice creams, if you prefer.

A   I was planning to make my own ice cream, but I'll have some panforte.
Can I pay by credit card?

B   Of course. Anything else?

A   No, I think that's everything. Thanks for your advice.

 Listen to more phrases and practise saying them: Track 14

Service with a smile

Excellent service!

If you need a service of some sort, or need help or information, these phrases will help you say what you want and ask for what you need.

Greetings

Use **Hello ...** as a general greeting to people in shops and banks, etc. It is polite to say **hello** to anyone in any situation.

> **Hello**, Madam.
> **Hello**, I wonder if you can help me.

Use **Hi ...** to greet people in more informal situations, for example a café or a hairdresser's.

> **Hi**, I'm seeing Freya for a haircut at 10:00.
> **Hi**, can I make a hair appointment?

You can use **Good morning, Good afternoon** or **Good evening** in slightly more formal situations, although to some people, this sounds slightly old-fashioned.

> **Good morning**. I'd like some advice on holiday insurance.

> **GOOD TO KNOW!**
> In English, there is no greeting starting with 'Good' that is for the whole day.

Use **Goodbye** when you leave a shop or bank, etc.

> Thanks for all your help. **Goodbye**.

Useful words

a haircut	an occasion when someone cuts your hair
an appointment	an arrangement to see someone at a particular time
insurance	an agreement that you make with a company in which you pay money to them regularly, and they pay you if something bad happens to you

Goodbye is often shortened to **Bye**. **Bye** is slightly informal.

> Thanks very much. **Bye**.

See you ... is a slightly informal way of saying goodbye, for example to a hairdresser that you know you will see again.

> Thanks very much. **See you** soon!
> Thanks, Louisa. **See you** in a couple of months.

People who work in shops often say **Have a good day!** or **Have a good weekend!** as you are leaving.

> Goodbye, **have a good day!**
> Bye, **have a good weekend!**

Talking about yourself

Often you will need to tell people information about yourself, such as your name and where you live. To say what your name is, use **My name is ...** .

> **My name is** Latif Keita.
> **My wife's name is** Astrid Backstrom.

To say where you live, use **my address is ...** .

> **My address is** 29 Kelvin Close, L3 0QT Liverpool.
> **My address** in New Zealand **is** 6 Green Street, Wellington.
> **My** permanent **address is** 7 avenue Foch in Aix.

Useful words
a couple   two or around two people or things
permanent   continuing forever or for a very long time

To say which country you were born in and lived in as a child, use **I'm from ...** .

> **I'm from** Algeria.
> **I'm from** Aberdeen in Scotland.
> **We're from** Bulgaria.

If you want to say that you are living somewhere for a short time, for example because you are on holiday, use **I'm staying ...** .

> **I'm staying** with a host family.
> **We're staying** in a rented house.

Saying what you have to do

To say what service or help you need, you can use **I have to ...** or **I need to ...** .

> **I have to** find out when they're going to deliver my television.
> **I have to** collect my jacket from the dry-cleaner's.

> **I need to** get my hair cut.
> **I need to** go to the optician's.

To ask what someone has to do, use **Do you have to ... ?** .

> **Do you have to** speak to someone at the bank?
> **Do you have to** show your passport?

Useful words

a host	someone who invites people to stay in their home
rented	used by people who pay money to the owner
find out	to learn the facts about something
deliver	to take something to a particular place
a dry-cleaner's	a shop where clothes are cleaned with a special chemical rather than water
an optician's	a shop where you can buy glasses

Another way of saying that it is important that you do something is **I must ...** .
This is used especially when it is *very* important that you do something.

> **I must** get my shoes mended.
> **I must** take some form of identification.

When you want to say that you should do something, use **I should ...** or
I ought to ... .

> **I should** visit the estate agent on my way home.
> **You should** rearrange the appointment.
> I suppose **I should** call them to cancel the appointment.
> **You shouldn't** throw it away before you've tried to get it mended.

> **I ought to** look online and see if I can find a cheaper deal.
> **You ought to** see if you can get it mended.
> **You ought to** write down the details of what they are offering.
> **We** really **ought to** find out about the service.

> **GOOD TO KNOW!**
> **Must/should + infinitive**
> The verb that comes after **must** or **should** is the infinitive without 'to'.

To say what you must not do, use **I mustn't ...** .

> **I mustn't** be late for my appointment.
> **I mustn't** forget that my suit is at the dry-cleaner's.
> **You mustn't** miss your appointment this time.

Useful words

identification	a document that proves who you are
an estate agent	a person whose job is to sell buildings or land
rearrange	to arrange for an event to happen at a different time
cancel	to say that something that has been planned will not happen
throw something away	to get rid of something that you do not want
online	using the Internet
a deal	a business agreement
details	the facts about someone or something

Saying what you want to do

The simplest way to say what you would like to do is to use **I'd like to ...** .

> **I'd like to** find out about the various accounts available.
> **I'd like to** transfer some money.
> **I'd like to** get this jacket dry-cleaned.

If you are very eager to do something, use **I'd really like to ...** or **I'd love to ...** .

> **I'd really like to** change my bank account.
> **I'd really like to** find out about other similar services.
> **I'd really like to** speak to someone who can advise me.

> **I'd love to** get my hair cut.
> **I'd love to** get some nice glasses.

A slightly informal way of saying that you would like to do or have something is **I wouldn't mind ...** .

> **I wouldn't mind** calling in at the bank on the way there.
> **I wouldn't mind** stopping off at the bank.

GOOD TO KNOW!
I wouldn't mind + -ing
The verb that comes after **I wouldn't mind ...** must be in the -ing form.

Useful words

various	of several different types
an account	an arrangement with a bank where they look after your money for you
transfer	to make something or someone go from one place to another
dry-clean	to clean clothes with a special chemical rather than water
advise	to tell someone what you think they should do
call in	to visit someone or something
stop off	to visit somewhere for a short time on your way to somewhere else

Asking for information

Use **Is ... ?** to ask general questions requiring information about things.

> **Is** the bank far from here?
> **Is** it far to the post office?

Use **Is there ... ?** or **Do you have ... ?** to ask whether something exists.

> Excuse me, **is there** a pharmacy near here?
> **Is there** an internet café in the area?

> **Do you have** any other types of accounts?
> **Do you have** an adviser that I can talk to?

To ask about the time that something will happen, use **What time ... ?** or **When ... ?**.

> **What time** does the bank shut?
> **What time** do I need to be here?

> **When** is the appointment?
> **When** shall I come back?

To ask about the price of something, use **How much ... ?**.

> **How much** is the service?
> **How much** is an eye test?
> **How much** do you charge to mend a pair of shoes?

Useful words

a pharmacy	a place where you can buy medicines
an Internet cafe	a café where there are computers which allow you to use the Internet
an adviser	an expert whose job is to give advice

To ask how much time something will take, use **How long ... ?**.

> **How long** is the appointment?
> **How long** do I have to wait to see someone?

To ask how to do something, use **How do you ... ?**.

> **How do you** open a bank account?
> **How do you** send money to the UK?

> **GOOD TO KNOW!**
> **How do you + infinitive**
> The verb that comes after **How do you ... ?** must be in the infinitive without 'to'.

Asking for things

To ask for something, use **Can I have ... ?**, **Could I have ... ?** or **I'd like ...** .
To be polite, use **please** at the beginning or end.

> **Can I have** a receipt, please?
> **Can I have** a photocopy of the document, please?
> Please **can I have** a brochure?

> **Could I have** a leaflet, please?
> **Could I have** some information, please?
> **Could I have** a list of prices, please?

Useful words

a bank account	an arrangement with a bank where they look after your money for you
a receipt	a piece of paper that shows you have received goods or money from someone
a photocopy	a copy of a document that you make using a special machine
a document	an official piece of paper with important information on it
a brochure	a thin magazine with pictures that gives you information about a product or a service
a leaflet	a piece of paper containing information about a particular subject

I'd like some advice, please.
I'd like an appointment next week, please.
I'd like your opinion.

If it is important for you to have something, you can use **I need ...** .

I need some help.
I need to get the money there quickly.
We need your signature.
You need some form of identification.

If you want to ask if something you want is available, use **Do you have ... ?** or **Do you do ... ?**.

Do you have your passport with you?
Do you have a fax machine?
Do you have your documents with you?

Do you do leaflets in English?
Do you do discounts for students?
Do you do hearing tests?

If you are asking someone if they can do something for you, the simplest way is to use **Can you ... ?** or **Could you ... ?**. **Could you ... ?** is slightly more polite and formal than **Can you ... ?**.

Can you call me when it's ready for collection, please?
Can you tell me how much it will be?

Could you send it to me by fax, please?
Could you have a look at my camera, please?

Useful words

a signature	your name written in your own special way
a fax machine	a special machine that is joined to a telephone line and that you use to send and receive documents
a discount	a reduction in the usual price of something
a fax	a special machine that is joined to a telephone line and that you use to send and receive documents

A polite way of asking someone to do something is by saying **Would you mind ... ?**.

> **Would you mind** giving me a photocopy of the contract?
> **Would you mind** giving me an estimate?
> **Would you mind** emailing me the details, please?

To ask whether something you want is possible, use **Is it possible ... ?**.

> **Is it possible** to get an earlier appointment?
> **Is it possible** to speak to the manager?
> **Is it possible** to pay in instalments?

Making suggestions

The simplest way to make a suggestion about what to do or buy is to use **You could ...** .

> **You could** come back tomorrow.
> **You could** find out the details online.
> Instead of buying a new one, **you could** repair your old one.

If two or more people are trying to decide what to do or buy, use **Shall we ... ?**.

> **Shall we** try a different hairdresser?
> **Shall we** come back later and see if they're open?
> **Shall we** ask for a refund?

Useful words

a contract	an official agreement between two companies or people
an estimate	a guess of how much you think something will cost
an instalment	one of several small regular payments that you make over a period of time
a refund	money that is returned to you because you have paid too much, or because you have returned goods to a shop

Use **How about ... ?** if you have an idea about what to do or buy.

> **How about** changing the appointment to Friday?
> **How about** asking to speak to the manager?
> **How about** changing your bank?

> **GOOD TO KNOW!**
> **How about + -ing**
> The verb that comes after **How about ... ?** must be in the -ing form.

Another way to make a suggestion is to say **Why don't ... ?**.

> **Why don't** you use the launderette on Elm Street?
> **Why don't** you get the TV mended?
> **Why don't** you exchange the bike for a bigger one?

I suggest ... and **You should ...** are slightly stronger ways of making a suggestion.

> **I suggest** you contact your bank in the US.
> **I suggest** you find a new cleaner.
> **I suggest** you get the locks on your doors replaced.

> **GOOD TO KNOW!**
> After **I suggest**, the verb that follows 'I/you/we, etc.' is the normal present tense. It should not have 'to' before it.

Useful words

a launderette	a place where people pay to use machines to wash and dry their clothes
exchange	to take something back to a shop and get a different thing
contact	to telephone someone or send them a message or a letter
a lock	the part of a door or container that you use to keep it shut and to make sure that no one can open it
replace	to get something new in the place of something that is damaged or lost

We should try to agree a price first.
We should open a savings account.
They should complain about the poor service.

Talking about your plans

Use **I'm + -ing verb** or **I'm going to ...** to talk about plans that you are sure of.

I'm getting a new key cut this morning.
She's meeting a financial adviser this afternoon to talk about her pension.

I'm going to change my hairdresser.
I'm going to complain about the service that we received.

To talk about your plans, you can also use **I'm planning to ...** or, if you are slightly less sure, **I'm hoping to ...** .

I'm planning to hire a dress for the occasion.
I'm planning to use caterers for the party.

I'm hoping to get to the optician's today.
She's hoping to get the bike mended.

Useful words	
savings	all the money that you have saved, especially in a bank
poor	bad
a key	a specially shaped piece of metal that opens or closes a lock
financial	relating to money
a pension	money that you regularly receive from a business or the government after you stop working because of your age
hire	to pay to use something for a short time
a caterer	a company that provides food and drink at an event such as a party

To talk about a plan that is only possible, use **I might ...** .

> **I might** have my hair and make-up done professionally.
> **I might** ask the florist's on the high street to do the flowers.

To talk about something that should happen in the future, use **I'm supposed to ...** .

> **I'm supposed to** provide original documents.
> What time **are we supposed to** be there?
> **He's supposed to** be paying for the service.

Useful words

make-up	the creams and powders that people put on their face to make themselves look attractive
professionally	by someone who does something as a job rather than for enjoyment
a florist's	a shop where you can buy flowers
original	not copied, but being the first

● Listen out for

Here are some phrases you are likely to hear in banks, hairdressers and other places that provide services.

Can I help you?
Can I help you at all?
Can I get you anything else?
Could I take a few details, please?
It'll be ready tomorrow.
It's not ready yet.
Do you have your receipt?
Do you need a receipt?
Remember to keep your receipts.
Do you have some form of identification?
Do you have your passport.
I'll need to see some form of identification.
What time of day would suit you best?
Do you have an appointment?
Please ring back tomorrow.
How would you like to pay?
Do you need a deposit?
I'll pay the full amount later.

Useful words

suit	to be convenient for you
a deposit	a sum of money that is part of the full price of something, and that you pay when you agree to buy it

Listen to the conversation: Track 15

Ashley is talking with an estate agent. She wants to find an apartment to rent.

A Hello, can I help you?

B Yes, I'm looking for an apartment to rent near the city centre.

A Certainly. I just need to take a few details first.

B Sure.

A Okay, what's your name, please?

B My name is Ashley Brook.

A And where do you live?

B My address is 12, Green Lane, Chorlton.

A And you would like to find an apartment in the city centre?

B That's right.

A What size apartment are you after?

B I'd really like one with three bedrooms, if that's possible.

A And when do you need this apartment for?

B I'm hoping to have somewhere by September as I'm starting a new job in the city in October.

A Right, let's see. How about this one? This has three bedrooms and is right in the centre.

B It's very nice but a bit expensive. Do you have anything a little bit cheaper?

A There's this one – it's cheaper but a bit smaller. It still has three bedrooms.

B That looks nice. Would you mind giving me the details of that, please? I'd like to show them to my friend before making any decisions.

A Of course. Why don't you take this away with you and get back to me when you've made a decision?

B That sounds good. Thanks a lot.

 Listen to more phrases and practise saying them: Track 16

Health

Get well soon!

If you become ill, have an accident or need other medical attention, the phrases in this chapter will allow you to talk to a doctor, dentist or pharmacist. Use them to get the advice or treatment that you need.

Describing the problem

If you need to describe a medical problem, you can use **I've got ...** .

> **I've got** a temperature.
> **I've got** a rash.
> **I have** high blood pressure.

If you want to say which part of your body hurts, use **My ... hurts**. If the pain you have is an ache, you can say which part of your body it is in by using **I've got a ... ache**.

> **My** back **hurts**.
> **His** foot **hurts**.
> **It hurts** here.

> **I've got** a head**ache**.
> **I've got** stomach**ache**.
> **She's got** tooth**ache**.

You can talk about more general problems that you are having using **I feel ...** .

> **I feel** tired all the time.
> **I'm feeling** better now.

Useful words
your temperature   how hot someone's body is
a rash   an area of red spots on your skin
your blood   the pressure at which blood flows around your body
  pressure

I've been feeling dizzy.
I've been feeling depressed.

If you want to tell a doctor about a problem you have, use **I'm ...** .

I'm allergic to penicillin.
I'm diabetic.
I'm on medication for my heart.

Saying what happened

If you have an accident, you will need to explain what happened. You will need to use a past tense, such as **I fell ...** or **I burnt ...** .

I bumped my head on a shelf.
I fell down the stairs.
She burnt herself on the stove.
I tripped over a kerb.

If your medical problem means that you cannot do something that you should be able to do, you can use **I can't ...** .

I can't put any weight on that foot.
I can't straighten my arm.
She can't bend her arm.

Useful words

dizzy	having the feeling that you are about to fall
depressed	feeling very sad for a long time
allergic	becoming ill when you eat, touch, or breathe something
penicillin	a type of medicine that kills bacteria
diabetic	having an illness where you cannot control the level of sugar in your blood
medication	medicine that is used for treating an illness
trip	to knock your foot against something and fall
a kerb	the edge of a pavement
straighten	to make something straight

If you hurt a part of your body as the result of an accident, you can use phrases such as **I've broken ...** or **I've sprained ...** to describe your injury.

> I think **I've broken** my arm.
> **She's broken** her toe.
> **I've sprained** my wrist.
> **I've twisted** my ankle.

Asking for information

When you need to get information about someone or something, you can use simple questions starting with **What ... ?**, **Which ... ?**, **How ... ?**, **Who ... ?** or **When ... ?**.

> **What** do I ask the pharmacist for?
> **Which** ward is she in?
> **How** do I make an appointment?
> **Who** did you see last time?
> **When** does visiting time start?

To ask where something is, use **Where can I find ... ?** . For more general information, you could say **Could you tell me ... ?** or **I'd like to know ...** . If you need to get someone's attention to ask a question like this, first say **excuse me**.

> Excuse me, **where can I find** a pharmacy?
> Excuse me, **where can I find** a dentist?
> Excuse me, **where can I find** a wheelchair?

Useful words

sprain	to injure a joint by suddenly stretching or turning it
twist your ankle	to injure your ankle (= the joint between your leg and your foot) by suddenly turning it
a pharmacist	a person whose job is to prepare and sell medicines
a ward	a room in a hospital that has beds for many people
a wheelchair	a chair with wheels that you use if you cannot walk very well

Could you tell me where the doctor's surgery is?
Could you tell me where to find the baby clinic?
Could you tell me what your symptoms are?

I'd like to know how long this will take.
I'd like to know where the eye department is.
I'd like to know what treatment you would recommend.

GOOD TO KNOW!

Notice that after **Could you tell me ...** and **I'd like to know ...**, the verb 'be' must come at the end of the sentence.

When you are speaking to a doctor or nurse, you may want to ask for advice from them. You can start your questions with **What's the best way ... ?**, **What would you recommend ... ?**, **What should I do ... ?** or **Could you give me some advice about/on ... ?** .

What's the best way to lose weight?
What's the best way of keeping your blood pressure under control?
What's the best way to treat depression?
What's the best way of keeping fit?

What would you recommend for a migraine?
What would you recommend for a bad cough?
What would you recommend for someone with flu?
What would you recommend to keep his temperature down?

Useful words

a surgery	the place where a doctor treats people
a clinic	a place where people receive medical advice or treatment
a symptom	something that is wrong with you that is a sign of a particular illness
recommend	to suggest that someone would find something good or useful
lose weight	to become thinner
depression	a state of mind in which you are very sad and you feel you cannot enjoy anything
a migraine	a very bad headache
flu	an illness that is like a very bad cold
a cough	when you suddenly force air out of your throat with a noise

What should I do if it happens again?
What should I do if it starts to bleed?
What should I do if the swelling gets worse?
What should I do if my children catch it?

Could you give me some advice on diet?
Could you give me some advice about eczema treatments?
Could you give him some advice on how to give up smoking?
Could you give him some advice about how to take the medicine?

Asking for things

When you want to find out if something is available, use **Have you got ... ?**.

Have you got anything for a headache?
Have you got anything for hay fever?
Have you got the doctor's phone number?

If you want to ask for something, start your sentence with **Can I have ... ?**.
To be polite, use **please** at the beginning or end of your sentence.

Can I have an appointment for tomorrow, please?
Can I have a packet of aspirins, please?
Please **can I have** a plaster?

Useful words

bleed	to lose blood from a part of your body
swelling	an area that is larger and thicker than normal
your diet	the food that you regularly eat
eczema	a medical condition which causes red, dry areas of skin
an aspirin	a medicine used to reduce pain and fever
a plaster	a small piece of sticky material used for covering small cuts on your body

If you want to buy something in a pharmacy, use **Can I have ... ?**, **I'd like ...** or **I'm looking for ...** . You can also say **I'm after ...** – this is slightly informal.

> **I'd like** some cough medicine, please.
> **I'd like** a toothbrush for a child.

> **I'm looking for** soap.
> **I'm looking for** some vitamins that are suitable for pregnant women.
> **I'm looking for** something to help with my indigestion.

> **I'm after** nappies.
> **I'm after** toothpaste.
> **I'm after** something that will help me sleep better.

Can I ... ? is used in sentences where you are asking if you are allowed to do something or if something is possible. If you want to be very polite, you can use **Is it possible ... ?** .

> **Can I** see the dentist this morning?
> **Can I** drive while I'm taking this medicine?

> **Is it possible** to see a different doctor?
> **Is it possible** to meet the surgeon before my operation?

Useful words

cotton wool	soft cotton material used for cleaning your skin
a vitamin	a substance in food that you need in order to stay healthy
indigestion	pains in your stomach because of something that you have eaten
a nappy	a piece of cloth or strong paper that a baby wears around its bottom
a surgeon	a doctor who is specially trained to do operations

If you are asking someone whether they can do something for you, you should use **Can you ... ?** or **Could you ... ?**, which is slightly more polite and formal. To be polite, you can use **please** at the beginning or end of these sentences. **Would you mind ... ?** is another polite way of asking someone to do something.

> **Can you** give me something for my earache, please?
> **Can you** send an ambulance straight away?

> **Could you** take us to the nearest hospital?
> **Could you** check my blood pressure?

> **Would you mind** changing this dressing for me?
> **Would you mind** passing me that bandage?

> **GOOD TO KNOW!**
> Notice that after **Would you mind ... ?** the verb always ends in -ing.

Saying what you want to do

A simple and polite way of saying what you want to do is by using **I'd like to ...** .

> **I'd like to** make an appointment with the doctor.
> **I'd like to** see a dentist as soon as possible.
> **I'd like to** talk to the pharmacist.

> **GOOD TO KNOW!**
> It is more polite to say **I'd like to** than simply 'I want to'.

Useful words
a dressing   a covering that protects an injury

Use **I'd prefer to ...** or **I'd rather ...** when you want to do one thing and not another. When you use **I'd rather ...**, note that if you want to mention the thing that you do not want, you should use **than** before it.

> **I'd prefer to** see a female doctor.
> **I'd prefer to** have the operation next week.
> **I'd prefer** not **to** take antibiotics.

> **I'd rather** have a private room.
> **I'd rather** see a physiotherapist.
> **I'd rather** take tablets **than** have an injection.

You can talk about things that it is important for you to do or to have by using **I need ...** .

> **I need** a prescription for my migraine tablets.
> **He needs** to see a doctor urgently.

Making suggestions

The most simple way to make a suggestion is to say **We could ...** or **Shall we ... ?**.

> **We could** get some tissues at the pharmacy.
> **You could** try and get an appointment tomorrow.

> **Shall we** call a doctor?
> **Shall we** put a bandage on it?

Useful words

antibiotics	medicine which cures infections by destroying harmful bacteria
a physiotherapist	someone whose job is to treat people who have injuries by moving parts of their body
an injection	medicine that someone puts into your body using a special needle
a prescription	a piece of paper on which a doctor writes an order for medicine
urgently	in a way that shows you need attention as soon as possible
a tissue	a piece of thin, soft paper that you use to wipe your nose

Another way to make a suggestion is to say **Why don't ... ?** or **Why not ... ?**.

> **Why don't** we ask for an appointment with the heart specialist?
> **Why don't** we ask the consultant for advice?
> **Why don't** you keep a diary of your symptoms?

> **Why not** see if you can take some time off work?
> **Why not** try an osteopath?
> **Why not** try cutting out milk from your diet?

How about ... ? is a slightly informal way of making suggestions of things to do or use.

> **How about** trying vitamin tablets?
> **How about** changing your diet a bit?
> **How about** walking to work instead of driving?

> **GOOD TO KNOW!**
> The verb that comes after **How about ... ?** must be in the -ing form.

Useful words

a specialist	a person who knows a lot about a particular subject
a consultant	someone who gives expert advice on a particular area of medicine
an osteopath	someone who treats injuries to bones and muscles
cut something out	to stop eating or drinking something
your diet	the type of food that you regularly eat

● Listen out for

Here are some useful phrases you are likely to hear or use at the doctor's or the hospital.

> How are you?
> What can I do for you?
> How long have you been feeling like this?
> Do you have any existing medical conditions?
> Are you on any other medication?
> Do you feel sick?
> Do you feel dizzy?
> Where does it hurt?
> Don't drink alcohol while you're taking this medicine.
> Please fill in this form.
> Can I have your medical insurance details?
> The results are fine.
> Are you allergic to antibiotics?
>
> My throat is very sore.
> I've been feeling nauseous.
> I've got a sharp pain in my side.
> I get out of breath very easily.
> I'm not sleeping well.
> I have no appetite.
> I'm getting a lot of headaches.

Listen to the conversation: Track 17

Brett has a skin problem and goes to a pharmacy to ask for advice.

A I wonder if you could help me? I've got a problem with my skin. I've got these sore patches behind my knees. They're dry and red, and they hurt if I touch them. Sometimes it gets so bad that I can't bend my legs.

B Do you mind if I have a look?

A Not at all. I'll just pull up my trouser leg.

B Hmm, yes. It looks like a small patch of eczema.

A Have you got anything that would make it better?

B You could try this cream – a lot of people find that it is very effective.

A How often should I put it on?

B Twice a day – once when you get up and again just before you go to bed.

A What about my diet? Can you give me any advice about that?

B Well, you could try cutting out dairy products for a while – sometimes that can help with eczema.

A Thanks, I'll try that. And what should I do if it doesn't go away?

B If it isn't getting better in a week or so, you should go and see your doctor.

 Listen to more phrases and practise saying them: Track 18

Help!

Don't worry!

If you find yourself in a situation in which you need help, for example if you have a problem, have an accident or lose something, use the following phrases.

Describing the problem

If you are asking somebody for help, you will need to be able to describe the problem. Use **There is ...** to say what the problem is. If the problem is that you do not have something you need, use **There isn't ...** .

> **There's** a smell of gas in my room.
> **There's** water all over the floor.
> **There's** smoke coming out of the engine.
> **There are** mice in the kitchen.

> **There isn't** any soap in the bathroom.
> **There isn't** enough food for everyone.
> **There isn't** any petrol in the car.

For some problems, you can use **I've got ...** .

> **I've got** a problem.
> **I've got** a flat tyre.
> **She's got** too much luggage to carry.
> **I've got** the wrong kind of plug for my laptop.

Useful words

smoke	the black or white clouds of gas that you see in the air when something burns
an engine	the part of a car that produces the power to make it move
petrol	the fuel which you use in cars and some other vehicles to make the engine go
a towel	a piece of thick soft cloth that you use to dry yourself
flat	with not enough air inside
a tyre	a thick round piece of rubber that fits around the wheels of cars and bicycles
luggage	the bags that you take with you when you travel
a plug	the plastic object with metal pins that connects a piece of electrical equipment to the electricity supply

If the problem is that you are not able to do something, use **I can't ...** .

> **I can't** turn the heating on.
> **I can't** get the car to start.
> **I can't** remember my password.
> **He can't** find his keys.

If you do not have the knowledge to do something, use **I don't know how to ...** .

> **I don't know how to** work this cooker.
> **I don't know how to** get my email.
> **We don't know how to** get there.
> **I don't know how to** change a fuse.

If a piece of equipment will not do what you want it to do, use **The ... won't ...** .

> **The** engine **won't** start.
> **The** cable **won't** reach the socket.
> **The** barbecue **won't** light.
> **The** shower **won't** work.

Useful words	
heating	the equipment that is used for keeping a building warm
a password	a secret word or phrase that allows you to use a computer system
a fuse	a small wire in a piece of electrical equipment that stops it from working when too much electricity passes through it
a cable	a thick wire that carries electricity
a socket	a hole that something fits into to make a connection
a barbecue	a piece of equipment that you use for cooking outdoors
light	to start something burning

Saying what happened

You will probably need to explain to somebody what happened. You can use
I've ... .

> **I've** forgotten my passport.
> **I've** had an accident.
> **We've** lost the key.
> **She's** broken her glasses.

To describe what someone else has done to you, use **I've been ...** . When you
don't know the person who did it, use **Someone ...** .

> **I've been** mugged.
> **We've been** burgled.
> **We've been** overcharged.
> **She's been** attacked.

> **Someone** stole my camera.
> **Someone** broke into the apartment while we were out.
> **Someone** took my bag while we were having dinner.
> **Someone** hit me on the back of the head.

Describing people and things

The simplest way to describe things that have been lost or stolen is using **It's ...** .

> **It's** a black Honda with red seats.
> **It's** a gold ring with three diamonds.

Useful words

mug	to attack someone and steal their money
burgle	to enter a building by force and steal things
overcharge	to charge someone to much for something
break in	to get into a building by force

When you are describing something, you may need to give more facts.
Use **It's made of ...** to say what it is made of.

> It's quite a small bag, and **it's made of** velvet.
> The beads are bright blue and **they're made of** glass.

To give more details about what something is like, use **It's got ...** .

> **It's got** a black handle.
> **It's got** my name inside it.
> **They've got** Chinese writing on them.

You may need to describe someone to the police, for example if they are lost or if you have seen them do something bad. Use **He's/She's got ...** to talk about what someone looks like.

> **She's got** short blond hair.
> **He's got** a beard.
> **She's got** a big nose.
> **They've** both **got** brown eyes.

To talk about someone's clothes, use **He's/She's wearing ...** .

> **She's wearing** jeans and a green T-shirt.
> **She's wearing** an orange blouse.
> **He's wearing** a black jacket.
> **They're wearing** swimming costumes.

Useful words

velvet	soft cloth that is thick on one side
a bead	a small piece of coloured glass, wood or plastic that is used for making jewellery
a handle	the part of a tool, a bag or a cup that you hold
blond	with pale-coloured hair
a blouse	a shirt for a girl or a woman
a swimming costume	a piece of clothing that is worn for swimming

Asking for information

You may need someone with a special skill to help you. Use **Is there ...** to ask about where to find them. You may need to get someone's attention before you can ask them a question. Use **Excuse me** to do this.

> Excuse me, **is there** a garage near here?
> **Is there** a police station near here?
> Excuse me, **are there** any public toilets near here?

If you want to know where to go to get help with your problem, use **Where can I find ... ?** .

> **Where can I find** someone to mend my watch?
> **Where can I find** information on how get oil stains out of clothes.
> **Where can I find** a good mechanic?

If you want someone to suggest someone or something that is good at fixing a problem, use **Can you recommend ... ?** .

> **Can you recommend** a good dry cleaner?
> **Can you recommend** a plumber?
> **Can you recommend** a wood polish for a scratched floor?

Useful words

a garage	a place where you can have your car repaired
a police station	the local office of the police in a particular area
a stain	a mark on something that is difficult to remove
a mechanic	a person whose job is to repair machines and engines, especially car engines
a dry cleaner	a shop where things can be cleaned with a special chemical rather than with water
a plumber	a person whose job is to put in and repair things like water and gas pipes, toilets and baths
polish	a substance that you put on a surface in order to clean it and make it shine

Use **Can you give me the number ...** to ask for the phone number of someone who can fix a problem.

> **Can you give me the number** of an electrician?
> **Can you give me the number** for the local police station?
> **Can you give me the number** of someone who can fix my chimney?

Asking for things

If you want to ask for something that will help with your problem, the simplest way is to use **Can I have ... ?** .

> **Can I have** the phone number of an electrician?
> **Can I have** another form, please?

If you want to find out if something is available, use **Do you have ... ?** .

> **Do you have** a sewing kit?
> Excuse me, **do you have** a lost property office?
> Excuse me, **do you have** this document in English?

Useful words

an electrician	a person whose job is to repair electrical equipment
a chimney	a pipe above a fire that lets the smoke travel up and out of the building
a form	a piece of paper with questions on it and spaces where you should write the answers
a sewing kit	the things you need to join pieces of cloth together
lost property	things that people have lost or accidentally left in a public place

If you are asking someone whether they can do something for you, you should use **Can you … ?** or **Could you … ?** . **Could you … ?** is slightly more polite and formal than **Can you … ?** . To be polite, you can use **please** at the beginning or end of these sentences.

> **Can you** help me, please?
> **Can you** call the police?

> **Could you** recommend an electrician?
> **Could you** show me how the shower works, please?

Use **Could I … ?** when you want to ask if you can do something that will help you with your problem.

> **Could I** use your phone?
> **Could I** borrow a ladder, please?
> **Could I** pay you back later?

Saying what you want to do

The simplest way to say what you want to do about your problem is to use **I'd like to …** . If you know that you do not want to do something, use **I don't want to …** .

> **I'd like to** make a complaint.
> **I'd like to** make a call.

> **I don't want to** stay in this room.
> **I don't want to** leave my car here.

Useful words

recommend	to suggest that someone would find a particular person or thing good or useful
a ladder	a piece of equipment made of two long pieces of wood or metal with short steps that is used for reaching high places
a complaint	when you say that you are not satisfied

Use **I'd rather ...** when you want to do one thing and not another. If you want to mention the thing that you do not want, you should use **than** before it.

> **I'd rather** hire a lawyer who can speak English.
> **We'd rather** read the documents in English, if possible.
> **I'd rather** have my money back **than** be given a replacement.

Saying what you have to do

If it is important for you to do something, use **I have to ...** or **I need to ...** .

> **I have to** go to the British embassy.
> **I have to** leave my room by eleven.
> **I have to** tell my wife that we're safe.

> **I need to** speak to my lawyer.
> **I need to** make a call.
> **I need to** call an electrician.

Making suggestions

The most simple way to make a suggestion is to say **We could ...** or **Shall we ... ?**.

> **We could** borrow some money.
> **You could** try switching it off and on again.

> **Shall we** call the police?
> **Shall we** try and fix it ourselves?

Useful words

a lawyer	a person whose job is to advise people about the law **a**
replacement	a person or thing that takes the place of another
an embassy	the building where people who represent a foreign country work

Another way to make a suggestion is to say **Why don't ... ?** or **Why not ... ?**.

> **Why don't** we tie it up with string?
> **Why don't** we see what the police officer says?
> **Why don't** you get a lift with Maria?

> **Why not** see if the garage can fix the car today?
> **Why not** see if you can get an earlier flight?
> **Why not** ask Ollie to lend you some tools?

> **GOOD TO KNOW!**
> **Why not + infinitive**
> The verb that comes after **Why not ... ?** must be in the infinitive form without 'to'.

Use **How about ... ?** if you have an idea about what to do about a problem.

> **How about** asking the people in the shop how it works?
> **How about** getting a bank loan?
> **How about** changing the oil?

> **GOOD TO KNOW!**
> **How about + -ing**
> The verb that comes after **How about ... ?** must be in the -ing form.

Useful words

tie	to fasten or fix something using string or a rope
string	very thin rope that is made of twisted threads
a lift	when you take someone somewhere in your car
a loan	an amount of money that you borrow

Talking about your plans

We often use **I'm + -ing verb** or **I'm going to ...** to talk about plans for dealing with problems.

> **I'm flying** out a day later than my husband.
> **I'm taking** it to the garage this afternoon.
> **We're seeing** our lawyer tomorrow.
> **We're changing** our electricity supplier.

> **I'm going to** phone the garage.
> **I'm going to** report the theft to the police.
> **I'm going to** call for help on my mobile.
> **We're going to** ask him to pay for the damage.

Use **Are you going to ... ?** or **Will you ... ?** to ask someone about their plans.

> **Are you going to** tow our car?
> **Are you going to** let Juan know what's happened?
> **Are you going to** change your ticket?
> **Are you going to** complain to the shop?

> **Will you** call us when it's ready?
> **Will you** mend the cover at the same time?
> **Will you** charge us extra for this?
> **Will you** be able to fix it?

Useful words

report	to tell people about something that happened
a theft	the crime of stealing
a mobile	a telephone that you can carry wherever you go
tow	to pull another vehicle along behind

150 help!

● Listen out for

Here are some key phrases you are likely to hear when you have some kind of problem.

What's the problem?
Is there anything I can do to help?
What's been taken?
Can I have your address, please?
Can I have your driving licence?
Were there any witnesses?
Have you reported it to the police?
Can I have your insurance details?
Please fill in this form.

I have a problem that I need help with.
Do you have a number for a taxi firm?
I urgently need to get in touch with my husband.
There's been an accident.
My car's broken down.
The shower/phone/radio doesn't work.
Could you mend my watch/shoes/bag?
Could you change the tyre/oil?
Is there someone here who can speak English?

Useful words

a driving licence	a document that shows that you have passed a driving test and that you are allowed to drive
a witness	a person who saw an event such as an accident or a crime
insurance	an agreement that you make with a company in which you pay money to them regularly; and they pay you if something bad happens to you or your property
details	the facts about something
urgently	in a way that needs attention as soon as possible
break down	to stop working

Listen to the conversation: Track 19

Emma's washing machine has broken down and water is leaking everywhere. She calls her landlord to ask what to do.

A I've got a problem with the washing machine. It suddenly stopped working, and now there's water all over the floor.

B Oh dear. Have you turned the water supply off?

A No, I don't know how to.

B There's a tap behind the washing machine. Turn that off and then call a plumber.

A Can you recommend one?

B I always use Mr Wilbur.

A OK, can you give me his number?

B It's 562 562. Why don't you write it down in case you need it again?

A Good idea. I'll call him straight away.

B OK. I'm coming round this afternoon anyway, so I'll help you clear up the mess.

Polly is on a work trip in America. She has just heard that her mother is very ill, and in hospital at home in Sheffield. She is trying to get an early flight back.

A Excuse me, I've got a problem that I need help with. I have a ticket for Saturday, but I've just heard that my mother is very ill, and I need to get home as soon as possible.

B I'm sure we can do something to help you. There's a flight at 3 or one tomorrow morning at 4 a.m. Shall I check if there are any seats on those?

A I'd rather go today, if possible.

B Let's see. Yes, you're lucky – there's one seat left on the 3 o'clock flight.

A Oh, that's great, thanks! Could I have a vegetarian meal?

B I'm sorry, it's too late to change the food arrangements now. Why not buy something in the café here to take with you?

A Good idea. Thanks very much for your help.

Listen to more phrases and practise saying them: Track 20

Telephoning and writing

Getting in touch

Talking on the phone is one of the hardest things to do in a foreign language, because you can't see the person you're speaking to, so you can't rely on body language and facial expressions to help you understand and communicate. This unit helps you to sound natural and confident when speaking on the telephone. It also shows you how to communicate by email, letter or text.

Making a telephone call

If you want to tell someone that you need to make a phone call, use **I need to ...** .

> **I need to** make a call
> Don't forget **you need to** call your mum back tonight.
> **I need to** top up my mobile.

To ask for a phone number, use **Do you have ... ?**.

> **Do you have** his home number, please?
> **Do you have** the number of a taxi firm?
> **Does she have** a mobile number?

You can also ask questions using **What ... ?** .

> **What**'s her extension number?
> **What**'s the code for the United States?
> **What** do I have to dial to get an outside line?

Useful words

top up a phone	to pay money so that you can make calls on your phone
a code	a group of numbers or letters that give information about something
an extension	a telephone that is connected to the main telephone in a building
dial	to press the buttons on a telephone in order to call someone
an outside line	a telephone line that connects you to someone outside the building you are in

When the person you're calling answers

Once you've made the call and someone answers, you will need to tell them who you are. Use **Hello, it's ... (here)** .

> **Hello** Mr Hall, **it's** Alex Ronaldson **here**.
> **Hello**, is Stéphanie in? **It's** Marie.

If the person you are ringing does not know you, or know who you are, use **Hello, my name is ...** . To explain more about who you are, use **I'm ...** .

> **Hello, my name is** Rosie Green. **I'm** a colleague of Peter's.
> **Hello, my name is** Lorna McCall. **I'm** Tanya Hill's assistant.

To check that you are speaking to the right person, use **Is that ... ?** .

> **Is that** Rolf?
> **Is that** the doctor's surgery?

If you want to ask for somebody, use **Is ... there?** or **Can I speak to ... ?**.

> **Is** Olivier **there**, please?
> **Are** your parents **there**?

> **Can I speak to** the manager, please?
> **Can I speak to** whoever's responsible for road safety?

GOOD TO KNOW!
If the person you want to speak to is not there, you may hear **Sorry, he's not here.** or **Sorry, she's not in.** . If the person is there, you may be asked **Who's calling, please?** If you hear this, you should say your name.

Useful words

an assistant	a person who helps someone in their work
a surgery	a place where a doctor sees patients
a manager	a person who controls all or part of a business or organisation
responsible	having the job or duty to deal with something

We often start a telephone conversation, especially with someone we know, by asking about their health, using **How are you?** .

> Hello, Otto. **How are you?**
> Hi, it's Chuck. **How are you?**
> **How is your brother?**

> **GOOD TO KNOW!**
> To answer that question, use **I'm fine, thanks.** or **I'm good thanks.** . If you are not well, you could say **Not great, really.** or **Not too good, actually.** .

You can start other general questions with **How's ... ?** .

> **How's** life?
> **How's** things with you?
> **How's** your job going?

Saying why you're calling

To say why you are calling, use **I'm phoning/calling/ringing about ...** or **I'm phoning/calling/ringing to ...** .

> **I'm phoning about** your advert for gardeners.
> **I'm calling about** Dad's birthday party.
> **I'm ringing about** the ballet classes.

> **I'm phoning to** arrange for our carpets to be cleaned.
> **I'm calling to** find out whether you sell garden furniture.
> **I'm ringing to** invite you and Stephanie over for dinner.

To explain where you are or what company or organisation you are from, use **I'm calling from ...** .

Useful words

an advert	information that tells you about something such as a product, an event, or a job
ballet	a type of dancing with carefully planned movements

I'm calling from the hotel.
I'm calling from the tax office.
I'm calling from the charity 'Help our Horses'.

If you want to ask whether you can do something, use **Can I ... ?** .

Can I charge up my phone here?
Can I use this to phone abroad?
Can I call him at work?

To ask someone else to do something, use **Could you ... ?** .

Could you give her a message, please?
Could you put me through to Johanna, please?
Could you ask him to call me back?

Giving information

When you make a phone call, you may be asked to give your own phone number. Use **My (phone) number is ...** .

My home phone number is ...
...and my mobile number is ...
My number at the university is ...

> **GOOD TO KNOW!**
> In English, we usually say the numbers separately, not as 'twenty five/forty three' etc. When there are two numbers the same next to each other, we say **double**. The number 0 is usually said like the letter 'O'. So the number 0223 would be said as 'O double two three'.

Useful words

a charity	an organisation that collects money for people or animals that need help
charge something up	to put electricity into something
put someone through	to connect someone to someone else on the telephone

To give details of where you can be contacted, use **You can contact me on ...** .

> **You can contact me on** 0998 02 46 23.
> **You can contact me on** my mobile.
> **You can contact me on** my sister's number.

Answering the telephone

> **GOOD TO KNOW!**
> It is very common to say **Hello?** when we answer the phone. At work, people sometimes answer by saying their name. Some people answer by saying their phone number, though this is rather old-fashioned.

If the person who is calling asks for you, say **Speaking.** .

> 'Can I speak to Lily, please?' '**Speaking**.'
> 'Is Ms Rathbone there, please?' 'Yes, **speaking**.'

To ask what the person calling wants to do, use **Would you like ... ?** .

> **Would you like** to leave a message?
> **Would you like** me to ask him to call you back?
> She's on another call at the moment. **Would you like** to hold?

To ask the person calling to do something, use **Would you mind ... ?** .

> **Would you mind** saying that again, please? I can't hear you very well.
> **Would you mind** spelling your name, please?
> **Would you mind** calling me back tomorrow?

Useful words

hold	to wait while still connected to the telephone until someone is free to speak to you
spell	to speak each letter of a word in the correct order

Ending a telephone call

When you end a telephone call, say **Goodbye.** in the same way as you would if you were leaving someone. This is often shortened to **Bye.** .

> Thanks for your help. **Goodbye**.
> OK then, **goodbye**.

> Right, **bye** Svetlana! Talk to you later!
> **Bye**, darling. See you soon.

To give someone good wishes for the next period of time, use **Have a good ... !** .

> **Have a good** day!
> **Have a good** weekend!
> **Have a good** holiday!

When you say goodbye, you may want to send your best wishes to someone else. In an informal situation use **Say hello to ...** , and in a more formal situation use **Give ... my best wishes.** .

> **Say hello to** your family.
> **Say hello to** your sister for me.

> **Give** your father **my best wishes**.
> **Give** Laura **my best wishes**.

Occasionally you may be forced to finish a call earlier than you had planned, especially on a mobile phone. To tell someone what the problem is, use **I don't have ...** .

> **I don't have** much charge left.
> **I don't have** any credit on my phone.

Useful words
charge	electricity
credit	money that is available to be spent on calls

● Listen out for

Here are some useful phrases you may hear when using the telephone.

Who's calling, please?

Who shall I say is calling?

Please hold the line.

Hang on a minute, I'll get him.

You've got the wrong number.

Do you have the extension number?

His line is engaged.

I'll put you through.

Please leave a message after the tone.

This call will cost 1 euro per minute.

All our operators are busy, please call back later.

You're breaking up.

Thanks for calling.

Useful words

hold the line	to wait on the telephone
an extension number	the number of a telephone that is connected to a main telephone in an organisation
engaged	already being used
put someone through	to connect you to someone else on the telephone
an operator	a person who connects telephone calls in a place such as an office or a hotel
break up	if a telephone line breaks up, you cannot hear the voices clearly

Writing letters and emails

Here are some useful phrases for writing letters and emails, and some examples of both.

> Dear Paul, …
> Hi Marta!
>
> Love, Naïma.
> Lots of love, Charlotte.
>
> All the best, Amandeep.
> Cheers, Lucien.
>
> Regards, Clive.
> Kind regards, Bella.
> Yours, Sujata.

To: miriam@ntlworld.com

Cc:

Subject: party for Stefan

Hi Dora!
Just a quick note to ask if you have any ideas about what to do for Stefan's party? I was thinking of having it in my flat, but I'm a bit worried about what the neighbours will think. Do you think we should hire a room somewhere?

Let me know what you think!

lots of love,
Miriam, x

GOOD TO KNOW!
When you say your email address, say 'at' for @ and 'dot' for . So this address is: miriam at ntlworld dot com.

63 Mill St
Churchby
CH4 7PN

— Your own address

14th February, 2015

— The date

Dear Dan

Thanks for the birthday card, and for your letter – your description of your brother falling in the sea made me cry with laughter!

I'm glad things are working out so well for you in Turkey. And that's one of the reasons I'm writing – I have two weeks holiday coming up, and I was thinking of coming to visit – what do you think?!?!

If it's not convenient, you must say, but it would be so great to see you and get to know your new friends.

Let me know soon!

Love,

Holly

PS Is there anything you want me to bring from England?

Use PS to add something to the end of a letter

Mr Andrew Kennedy
37 Church Rd
Glasgow
G64 3PH
UK

The postcode
comes after
the name of
the town

Starting a formal letter or email

Dear Mr Surplice, ...
Dear Prof Amies, ...
Dear Sir or Madam, ...

GOOD TO KNOW!
It is very old-fashioned to use **Dear Sir** only if you do not know whether
the person you are writing to is a man or a woman, and it could cause
offence. Use **Dear Sir or Madam** or even something like **Dear Neighbours**
or **Dear Parents**, according to the reason you are writing.

Ending a formal letter or email

Yours faithfully, Anton Smit
Yours sincerely, Ali Sharpe

GOOD TO KNOW!
We use **Yours sincerely** to end a letter where we have used the person's
name, and **Yours faithfully** where we did not use the name, but
something like 'Dear Sir/Madam'.

Ending a formal letter or email in a slightly more friendly way

Best wishes, Valentina Clark
Kind regards, Tony Bishop

17 King St
Liverpool
LP29 6AG

— Your own
address

Mrs A Hughes
Staffords Accountancy
Unit 13
Hopetown Business Park
DP2 4AL

— Name and
address of
the person/
company you
are writing to

2 June 2014

— The date

Dear Mrs Hughes,

I am writing to apply for the job of part-time
receptionist with your company. I saw your
advert in the *Hopetown Times*.

I am currently working as a receptionist for
a legal firm in Grisham, but I would like to find
a job closer to home.

I enclose my CV and look forward to hearing
from you.

Yours sincerely,

Karen Miller

Karen Miller

Texting

Texting is a very popular and quick way to communicate. We often use special abbreviations for texting. Here are some common ones. Some people write them using capital letters.

@	at	lo	hello
2	to *or* two	lol	laughing out loud
2day	today	m8	mate
2moro	tomorrow	pls	please
4	for	pov	point of view
aml	all my love	r	are
asap	as soon as possible	rofl	rolling on the floor laughing
atm	at the moment	some1	someone
b4	before	soz/sry	sorry
btw	by the way	spk	speak
c	see	syl	see you later
cm	call me	tx/thx	thanks
cu	see you	u	you
cul	see you later	ur	your/you're
fyi	for your information	w8	wait
gr8	great	wan2	want to
ic	I see	wk	week
im(h)o	in my (humble) opinion	wrk	work
l8	late	xlnt	excellent
l8r	later	y	why

Listen to the conversation: Track 21

Jim is trying to phone the finance manager of a large company.

A Good morning. Fletcher and Smith Finance. How can I help you?

B Could I speak to Ava Watts, please?

A Certainly. Who shall I say is calling?

B My name is Jim Allsop. I'm ringing from Hector's Ltd to discuss our credit arrangements.

A Thank you. I'll put you through. Oh, I'm sorry – she's on another line at the moment. Do you mind if I put you on hold?

B I'm rather busy, actually. Could you ask her to call me back later?

A No problem. Can you give me your number?

B My office number is 01223 513 656, and the extension is 56. If I'm not there, she can contact me on my mobile – I think she has the number already.

A Thank you very much. I'll give her that message.

B Thank you. Goodbye.

Emma is phoning her friend Ashley for a chat.

A Hello ?

B Hi, Ashley. It's Emma.

A Emma! Great to hear from you – how's things with you ?

B Really good, thanks. I've got a new flat now, so I was calling to see if you want to come over some time?

A   Oh, I'd really love to, but I've got my exams next week, and then I'm moving to a new place myself.

B   OK, we'd better leave it until after that, then. Will you still be on this phone number?

A   No, but you can contact me on my mobile.

B   OK, then. Good luck with your exams.

A   Thanks for calling. And say hello to Lara for me!

B   I will. Bye for now.

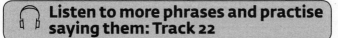

Listen to more phrases and practise saying them: Track 22

Work

At work

Most types of work involve a lot of speaking. Whether you are discussing a project, making a telephone call to a customer or arranging a meeting, you will need to say a variety of things to your colleagues. These phrases will help you to talk naturally and confidently in a work situation.

Greetings

Many types of work involve meeting people that you do not know. To tell someone you have just met your name, use **Hello, I'm ...** .

>**Hello, I'm** Carlos Sanchez.
>**Hello, I'm** Lanying Peng.

If a person tells you their name, reply by saying **Pleased to meet you.** Then tell them your name by first saying **I'm ...** .

>**Pleased to meet you. I'm** Carole Durand.
>**Pleased to meet you. I'm** Curt Haussman.

You may also want to tell the person what your job is in the company that you work for. To do this, say **I'm ...** .

>**I'm** the marketing manager for the UK.
>**I'm** the head of sales for Western Europe.
>**I'm** in charge of human resources at Went International.

Useful words

a customer	someone who buys something from a shop or website
a colleague	a person someone works with
marketing	the advertising and selling of products
a manager	a person who controls all or part of a business or organisation
a head	the person who is in charge of a company or organisation
in charge of someone/ something	responsible for someone or something
human resources	the part of a company that employs and trains people and deals with people who have problems

Introducing people

You may want to introduce a new person to a colleague. The simplest way to do this is to say **This is ...** giving the person's full name after.

> Leila, **this is** Chen Wang.
> Charlotte, **this is** Anna-Maria Delgado. Anna-Maria, **this is** Charlotte Walker.

Another way of introducing two people, especially if you are not sure whether they have met before, is to start by saying **Have you met ... ?**. If the two people have not met, you can then introduce them as above.

> Lucia, **have you met** Jin?
> Daiki, **have you met** Abdul? Abdul, this is Daiki Suzuki.
> Carina, **have you met** Bruno? Bruno, this is Carina Edberg.

Talking about your plans

When you are with your colleagues, you will want to talk about things that you will definitely do that day, that week, that month, etc. For plans like these that you are sure of, you can use **I'm + -ing verb**.

> **I'm seeing** a colleague here in half an hour.
> **She's attending** a conference in Madrid next week.
> **I'm meeting** Carlo and Johannes tomorrow to discuss the issue.

Useful words

introduce	to tell people each other's names so that they can get to know each other
attend	to be present at an event
a conference	a long meeting about a particular subject
discuss	to talk about something
an issue	an important subject that people are talking about

For plans that you are sure of, you can also use **I'm going to ...** .

> **I'm going to** email Faisal this morning to let him know.
> **I'm going to** call the Spanish office today to ask their opinion.
> **We're going to** meet Channa to talk about book sales.

To talk about your plans, you can also use **I plan to ...** or **I intend to ...** .

> **I plan to** have the work finished by the end of next week.
> **I plan to** visit the Spanish office in June.
> **I plan to** hold a series of meetings to discuss the matter.

> **I intend to** consult all the managers before making any decisions.
> **I intend to** work on the report this Friday.
> **I intend to** circulate the document among the managers first.

If you want to talk about a plan that you are not completely sure about, you can use **I hope to ...** .

> **I hope to** finish the report this week.
> **I hope to** meet with Francine while I'm in Amsterdam.
> **We hope to** complete the project by December 12th.

To talk about what should happen in the future, use **I'm supposed to ...** .

> **I'm supposed to** send the figures to Adam today.
> **I'm supposed to** be talking at the conference.
> What time **are we supposed to** meet them?
> **He's supposed to** be calling me this morning.

Useful words

a series	a number of things or events that come one after another
a matter	something that you must talk about or do
consult	to ask someone for their advice
a report	a piece of work that is written on a particular subject
circulate	to send something to all the people in a group
a document	a piece of text that is stored on a computer

Making suggestions

To say to a colleague that you will do something, use **I can ...** or **I'll ...** .

> **I can** check these figures.
> **I can** speak to Adriana, if you like.
> **I can** ask him, if you like.

> **I'll** order more stationery.
> **I'll** email Santiago, if you like.
> **I'll** send you a copy, if you like.

> **GOOD TO KNOW!**
> When people use **I can ...** or **I'll ...** to say they will do something, they often add **if you like** at the end of the sentence.

To suggest something that you and your colleagues could do, use **we could ...** .

> **We could** cancel the contract.
> **We could** refuse to pay them.
> **We could** offer the job to someone else.

Another way to suggest something that you and your colleagues could do is **Shall we ... ?**.

> **Shall we** postpone the meeting?
> **Shall we** discuss this with Natalia?
> **Shall we** tell the staff?

Useful words

check	to make sure that something is correct
order	to ask for something to be sent you from a company
stationery	paper, envelopes and other materials or equipment used for writing or typing
a copy	something that is produced that looks exactly like another thing
cancel	to say that something that has been planned will not happen
a contract	an official agreement between two companies or people
postpone	to arrange for an event to happen at a later time
staff	the people who work for an organization

Asking for suggestions

The simplest way of asking a colleague for advice is **Should I … ?**.

> **Should I** ask Domenico first?
> **Should I** send a copy of the letter to Lars?
> **Should I** forward this email to Hualing?

Another way of asking for advice is **Do you think I should … ?**.

> **Do you think I should** set up a meeting?
> **Do you think I should** tell my boss?
> **Do you think we should** employ someone else?

If you are asking a colleague whether they think something is good and should be used, say **Would you recommend … ?**.

> **Would you recommend** advertising in the paper?
> **Would you recommend** the service that they provide?
> **Would you recommend** taking a client there for lunch?

Saying what you have to do

To tell your colleagues that it is very important that you do something, use **I have to …** or **I need to …** .

> **I have to** email Cyrus and ask him.
> I really **have to** finish this piece of work today.

Useful words

forward	to send a letter or an email to someone after you have received it
set up something	to arrange something
a boss	the person in charge of you at the place where you work
employ	to pay someone to work for a person or a company
advertise	to tell people about something in newspapers, on television, on signs, or on the Internet
a service	the help that people in a shop, restaurant or company give you
a client	a person who pays someone for a service

You **have to** call the customer when the goods are ready.
You don't **have to** work till eight o'clock every evening.

I **need to** call our supplier.
I **need to** cancel that order.
We **need to** work more quickly.

To ask what someone has to do, use **Do you have to ... ?** .

Do you have to dress smartly for the office?
Do you have to get to work for nine o'clock?
Do you have to have lunch with your colleagues?

Another way of saying that it is important that you do something is **I must ...** .
This is used especially when it is *very* important that you do something.

I must send that fax to Vincenzo.
You must write down the customer's telephone number.
We must find someone else to do the work.

> **GOOD TO KNOW!**
> There is no 'to' after **I must ...** .

Use **I should ...** or **I ought to ...** to say what is the right thing to do, even if you are not going to do it.

I should call Sergei and let him know.
I should offer her the job first.
We really **should** pay him the same as Jamila.

Useful words	
goods	things that you can buy or sell
a supplier	a company that sells something such as goods or equipment to customers
an order	the thing that someone has asked for
smartly	in a clean and tidy way
a fax	a copy of a document that you send or receive using a special machine that is joined to a telephone line
let someone know	to tell someone about something

I **ought to** ask human resources what they think.
I **ought to** send that contract back today.
We ought to pay Walkers for the work they've done.

> **GOOD TO KNOW!**
> There is no 'to' after **I should ...** .

Asking for things

To ask a colleague if you can have something, use **Can I ... ?** or **Could I ... ?**.
Could I ... ? is slightly more polite and formal than **Can I ... ?**. To be polite,
use **please** at the beginning or end of these sentences.

Can I use your mobile, please?
Can I see those figures, please?
Can I come to the meeting?

Could I see that document, please?
Could I use your laptop?
Could I have a copy of that document, please?

To ask a colleague if they can do something for you, use **Can you ... ?** or **Could
you ... ?**.

Can you ask Birgit to call me, please?
Can you take a message for me, please?
Can you get me those figures, please?

Could you send me that report, please?
Could you speak to Jingfei about the problem?
Could you get the report to me by next Wednesday, please?

Useful words
a laptop   a small computer that you can carry with you

A very polite way to ask a colleague if they can do something for you is to use **Would you mind + -ing?**.

> **Would you mind contacting** the suppliers?
> **Would you mind taking** the minutes at the next meeting?
> **Would you mind writing** an agenda for the meeting?

If it is important for you to have something, you can use **I need ...** .

> I really **need** the information now.
> **We need** a supplier that we can trust.
> We're so busy **we need** extra staff.

Apologizing

Sometimes when we are at work, there are problems and we make mistakes. When this happens we may need to say we are sorry to a colleague or a customer. To apologize, use **I'm sorry ...** or **Sorry ...** .

> **I'm sorry** if you didn't get the attachment with the email.
> **I'm sorry** I was late for the meeting.

> **Sorry** – I don't have a copy of the agenda.
> **Sorry**, I didn't hear what you were saying.

If you have to tell a colleague or a customer that there is a problem or that something bad has happened, start your sentence with **I'm afraid ...** .

> **I'm afraid** I can't come to the meeting.
> **I'm afraid** there's a problem with your order.

Useful words

contact	to telephone someone or send them a message or letter
take the minutes	to write what is said and decided at a formal meeting
an agenda	a list of things to be discussed at a meeting
busy	having a lot of things to do
an attachment	a file that is attached to an email message and sent with it
an agenda	a list of things to be discussed at a meeting

A more formal way of saying that you are sorry is to use **My apologies ...** .

> **My apologies** – I forgot to send you the memo.
> **My apologies** – my train was delayed.
> **My apologies** – that was my fault.

> **GOOD TO KNOW!**
> If someone apologizes to you, reply **That's all right**. or **Don't worry**.
> This lets the person who is apologizing know that you are not angry
> with them or that the problem is not important.

Expressing opinions

If you want to give your opinion about something, use **I think ...** .

> **I think** their website is excellent.
> **I think** she's very good at giving presentations.
> **I don't think** they did a very good job.
> **I thought** she was the best candidate.

You can also give your opinion of something by saying **in my opinion ...** .

> **In my opinion**, these targets are too high.
> **In my opinion**, she's in the wrong job.

Useful words

a memo	a short note that you send to a person who works with you
delay	to make someone or something late
someone's fault	something bad that you have caused to happen
a website	a set of information about a particular subject that is available on the internet
a presentation	an occasion when someone shows or explains something to a group of people
a candidate	someone who is trying to get a particular job
a target	the result that you are trying to achieve

To ask someone for their opinion, say **What do you think of ... ?**.

> **What do you think of** their products?
> **What do you think of** that strategy?

You can also ask someone for their opinion by saying **What's your opinion of ... ?**.

> **What's your opinion of** the competition?
> **What's your opinion of** their performance?

Agreeing and disagreeing

If you think that what someone has said is right, say **I agree ...** .

> **I agree**. I think it's been a very successful project.
> Yes, **I agree** with you. We need to promote her.

You can also agree with what someone has said by saying **You're right ...** .

> **You're right.** Profits have declined.
> I think **you're right** about the website.

If you feel strongly that what someone has said is right, say **I totally agree ...** .

> **I totally agree**. I think she's an excellent leader.
> **I totally agree** with you, James.

Useful words

a strategy	a general plan or set of plans for the future
the competition	the company or person that you are competing against
a performance	how well someone does something
successful	doing or getting what you wanted
promote	to give someone a more important job in the same organization
a profit	the amount of money that you gain when you sell something for more money than you paid for it
decline	to become less in amount
a leader	the person who is in charge of a group of people or an organization

If you think that what someone has said is wrong, say **I disagree ...** .

> **I disagree**. I've always found her to be very efficient.
> **I disagree** with you here.
> I'm afraid I **disagree**.

If you feel strongly that what someone has said is wrong, say **I totally disagree ...** .

> **I totally disagree**. I think we've spent too much already on this project.
> I'm afraid **I totally disagree** with you here.

> **GOOD TO KNOW!**
> When people say **I disagree**, they often start the sentence with
> **I'm afraid**. This sounds more polite and less forceful.

● Listen out for

Here are some important phrases you are likely to use and hear at work.

> We need to arrange a meeting to discuss this.
> Svetlana sends her apologies.
> Could someone take the minutes for the meeting?
> What's next on the agenda?
> Could you put together an agenda for the meeting?

> How do you switch this on?
> Where can I plug this in?
> My computer has crashed again.
> I'll just start up my computer.
> I don't have any record of that.
> I've forgotten my password.

Useful words

efficient	able to do tasks successfully, without wasting time or energy
put together	to organize something
a password	a secret word or phrase that allows you to enter a place or use a computer system

Could you forward me that email?
I sent it as an attachment.
I can't open the attachment.
Could I have a brief chat with you?
Do you have a moment?
I'll have a word with him.

She's applied for another job.
She's leaving the company.
He's been promoted.
He's resigned.
She's retiring at the end of the year.

Useful words

brief	lasting only a short time
a chat	a conversation
a moment	a short amount of time
have a word with someone	to speak to someone
apply	to write a letter or write on a form in order to ask for something such as a job
resign	to tell your employer that you are leaving
retire	to leave your job and usually stop working completely

Listen to the conversation: Track 23

Annabel is telling her colleague Peter about a work trip that she is planning. It will be the first time she has travelled on business. Peter has travelled a lot in his job so he is able to offer Annabel advice.

A   So where are you going on your trip?

B   I'm meeting some clients in Paris and then I'm travelling on to Madrid for a conference.

A   That sounds exciting! Are you going to stay in the centre of Paris?

B   Well, I hope to, if I can find a hotel that's not too expensive – and not booked up. I think that might be difficult at this time of the year.

A   Yes, it might be. I can give you the names of a couple of places where I've stayed in the centre of Paris. I'll email you the addresses when I get back to my desk.

B   Oh, thanks, that would be great. Would you recommend meeting clients in the hotel itself – or should I find a café somewhere where we can meet up?

A   I don't think it matters. You just need to find somewhere quiet where you can sit down and talk without being disturbed.

B   Yes, that's the main thing. I must book my hotels soon. I'm going in three weeks.

A   Yes, do. Just out of interest, who are you meeting in Paris?

B   A couple of clients – Philippe Blanc and Kevin Henri. Do you know them?

A   Yes, I do, as it happens.

B   Ah, that's interesting. What do you think of Philippe?

A He's all right but you have to be quite firm with him. He tends to get what he wants out of a meeting.

B You're making me nervous! Do you think I should practise what I'm going to say with one of my colleagues here?

A Yes, why not?

B If you have a couple of minutes later this week, would you mind listening to what I plan to say?

A Not at all – I'd be pleased to. How about this afternoon? I'm free after 3 o'clock. Just give me a call when you're ready.

B That's fantastic. Thank you so much.

 Listen to more phrases and practise saying them: Track 24

studying

Academic life

If you are at school, college, or university, the phrases in this section will allow you to talk about your studies. You will be able to use them in discussions in class, as well as for finding information you need and expressing your own opinions about the subjects you are studying.

Asking for information

When you need to get information about something, make questions with words such as **What ... ?, Where ... ?** or **When ... ?**.

> **What** are we studying this term?
> **What** room is the lecture in?
> **Where** is the gym?
> **Where** can I get a library card?
> **When** is your first lecture?
> **When** do we have to hand in our essays?

A polite way to ask for general information is **Could you tell me ... ?** .

> **Could you tell me** where Professor Nentwich's office is, please?
> **Could you tell me** how to use this microscope?
> **Could you tell me** what time the library opens?

Useful words	
a lecture	a talk that someone gives in order to teach people about a particular subject
a gym	a club, building or large room with equipment for doing physical exercises
hand something in	to take something to someone and give it to them
an essay	a short piece of writing on a subject
a microscope	a scientific instrument that makes very small objects look bigger

Use **Is there ... ?** or **Are there any ... ?** to ask whether something exists.
You use these phrases especially when you want to have something to use.

> **Is there** any paper left?
> **Is there** a spare laptop in here?
> **Are there** any pens in that box?
> **Are there** any more calculators?

A very common way of asking how to do something is to use the phrase
How do you ... ?. You could also say **What's the best way ... ?** .

> **How do you** spell that?
> **How do you** divide a small number by a bigger number?
> **How do you** turn this computer on?

> **What's the best way** to improve my English pronunciation?
> **What's the best way** of preparing for the exam?
> **What's the best way** of recording the results of our experiment?

If you want to ask someone for advice about your studies, use **Could you give
me some advice ... ?** . This phrase is followed by the prepositions **about** or **on**.

> **Could you give me some advice** about what background reading
>   I should be doing?
> **Could you give me some advice** on how to organise my essay?
> **Could you give me some advice** about revision techniques?

Useful words

spare	not being used by anyone else
a calculator	a small electronic machine that you use to calculate numbers
pronunciation	the way that you say a word
background reading	reading that you do to learn general facts about a subject you are studying
revision	when you study something again in order to prepare for an exam
a technique	a special way of doing something practical

Expressing opinions

You will probably be asked to give your opinions about things you are studying. The simplest way is to use **I think ...** .

> **I think** this reading list is rather out of date.
> I really **think** that the only way to learn a language properly is to live in the country.
> **I don't think** we're doing much algebra this term.

You can also use **In my opinion ...** . This is a strong way to express your opinion, and is more suitable in a formal discussion in class than with friends.

> **In my opinion**, global warming is caused by humans.
> **In my opinion**, his views about women are very old fashioned.
> **In my opinion**, Galileo is still the greatest astronomer who ever lived.

To talk about someone else's opinion, you can use **According to ...** . This phrase is also more suitable in a formal discussion in class than with friends. You could also use **Some people say ...** , which is less formal.

> **According to** Virginia Woolf, every woman needs a room of her own.
> **According to** the latest research, genes play an important role in the disease.
> **According to** my tutor, the exam is more difficult now than it used to be.

Useful words	
a reading list	a list of books on a particular subject that students are asked to read
algebra	a type of mathematics in which letters and signs are used to represent numbers
global warming	the gradual rise in the Earth's temperature caused by high levels of certain gases
an astronomer	someone who studies the stars, planets and other natural objects in space
research	when someone studies something and tries to discover facts about it
a gene	the part of a cell that controls a person's, an animal's or a plant's physical characteristics, growth and development
a role	what someone or something does in a situation
a tutor	someone who gives lessons to one person or a very small group of people

> **GOOD TO KNOW!**
> When you use **According to ...,** you must always follow it with the name of someone or something else – we do not say 'According to me'.

Some people say that Shakespeare did not really write those plays.
Some people say her early works are better.
Some people say Mozart was the greatest composer who ever lived.

If you want to ask other people their opinion of something, use **What do you think of ... ?** or **What do you think about ... ?**.

What do you think of the new language labs?
What do you think of his book on Marx?

What do you think about Picasso's use of colour in this painting?
What do you think about setting up a French conversation group?

To agree with someone's opinion, use **I agree.** or **You're right..** If you want to say who you agree with, use **with**.

'This book is really useful.' '**I agree**. I used it a lot when I was writing my essay.'
I agree with Ana that we need more help with our revision.
I completely **agree with** you!

'I think this chemical must be sulphur.' '**You're right**.'
He's right that business studies is a useful subject.

Useful words

a composer	a person who writes music
a language lab	a room containing equipment for learning languages
sulphur	a yellow chemical that has an unpleasant smell
business studies	the study of how businesses work

If you do not agree with someone, you can use **I don't agree.** This is quite strong, so to be more polite, you might say **I'm afraid I don't agree.** or **I don't really agree.**

'What a great lecture.' '**I don't agree.** She didn't tell us anything new.'
'I think Dostoevski is the greatest psychologist in literature.' '**I'm afraid I don't agree.** For me, it has to be Proust.'
'Media studies is just a waste of time.' '**I don't really agree.** It teaches you a lot about analysing what you see.'

Another strong way of saying that you do not agree is **I disagree.** .

'Nabokov is a men's writer.' '**I disagree**. I know lots of women who admire his work.'
'He says most people are honest.' 'Well, **I disagree** with him on that.'
'Churchill was Britain's greatest Prime Minister.' 'I strongly **disagree**.'

Asking for and giving explanations

You will often need to ask your teacher to explain things. The simplest way is to use **Why ... ?** .

Why do we need protein in order to grow?
Why can't we use calculators in the exam?
Why did the Egyptians build pyramids?

Useful words

a psychologist	someone who studies the human mind and the reasons for people's behaviour
media studies	the study of newspapers, televisions, advertising, etc.
analyse	to consider something carefully in order to fully understand it or to find out what is in it
admire	to like and respect someone or something very much
honest	always telling the truth and not stealing or cheating
the prime minister	the leader of the government in some countries
protein	a substance that the body needs that is found in meat, eggs, fish and milk
a calculator	a small electronic machine that you use to calculate numbers
a pyramid	a solid shape with a flat base and flat sides that form a point where they meet

Could you explain ... ? can be used to ask your teacher to explain something.
Your teacher might use it to ask you to explain something too.

> **Could you explain** how a liquid can change into a gas?
> **Could you explain** how volcanos are formed?
> **Could you explain** why women weren't allowed to vote?
> **Could you explain** why you came to this conclusion?

To ask for a reason, use **What is the reason ... ?** .

> **What is the reason** for the change in temperature?
> **What was the reason** for Nelson Mandela's imprisonment?
> **What was the reason** for Shylock's anger in this scene?

A slightly more informal way of asking for an explanation is **Why is it that ... ?** .

> **Why is it that** we're not studying Freud in psychology?
> **Why is it that** the glacier doesn't melt?
> **Why was it that** they lost that battle?

The simplest way of giving an explanation is to use **Because ...** .

> **Because** many babies died at that time.
> Your answer was not correct **because** you put the decimal point in
>   the wrong place.
> **Because** heat cannot pass from a colder object to a warmer object.

Useful words

a volcano	a mountain that throws out hot liquid rock and fire
vote	to show your choice officially at a meeting or in an election
a conclusion	a decision that you make after thinking carefully about something
imprisonment	when someone is put in prison
psychology	the study of the mind and the reasons for people's behaviour
a glacier	a very large amount of ice that moves very slowly, usually down a mountain
a battle	a fight between armies during a war
a decimal point	the dot that you use when you write a number as a decimal

> **GOOD TO KNOW!**
> In speech, it is fine to use **because** at the beginning of a sentence, although it is not considered good style to do this in writing.

You can also use **The reason is that ...** .

> **The reason is that** trees absorb the carbon dioxide.
> **The reason is that** the second number is larger than the first.
> **The reason is that** mountains formed a natural barrier between them.

Explaining a problem

To explain a general problem, use **I've got a problem ...** . Use the preposition **with** to talk about a thing that is causing your problem.

> **I've got a problem** – I want to do French and history, but the classes are at the same time.
> **I've got a problem with** my essay – it's too long and I don't know what to cut out.
> **I've got a problem with** my laptop.

To talk about something that has happened that is causing you a problem, use **I've** with a past participle.

> **I've lost** my notes.
> **I've forgotten** to bring my homework.
> **I've messed up** the experiment.

If someone else has caused your problem, use **Someone's** with a past participle.

> **Someone's spilled** coffee all over my essay.
> **Someone's stolen** my laptop.

Useful words

absorb	to take in a substance
carbon dioxide	a gas that animals and people produce when they breathe out
a barrier	a fence or a wall that prevents people or things from moving from one area to another

If you do not know how to do something, use **I don't know how to ...** .

> **I don't know how to** measure the flow of electricity.
> **I don't know how to** set up the equipment.
> **I don't know how to** find the original reference.

If your problem is that you do not have something that you need, use **There isn't ...** or **There aren't ...** .

> **There isn't** a projector in this room.
> **There wasn't** enough time to ask questions.
> **There aren't** enough handouts for everyone.
> **There weren't** any aprons in the cupboard.

Asking for permission

The simplest way to ask your teacher or lecturer for permission to do something is to use **Can I ... ?**.

> **Can I** send you a draft of my essay?
> **Can I** use this microscope?
> **Can we** look at the answers now?

Useful words

flow	when something moves somewhere in a steady and continuous way
set something up	to start or arrange something
original	used for talking about something that existed at the beginning
a reference	the name of the person who said or wrote something and the place where they said or wrote it
a projector	a machine that shows films or pictures on a screen or on a wall
a handout	a piece of paper containing information that is given to people in a meeting or a class
an apron	a piece of clothing that you wear over the front of your normal clothes, especially when you are cooking, in order to prevent your clothes from getting dirty.

To ask if your teacher is happy for you to do something, use **Is it OK … ?** or **Do you mind if … ?** .

> **Is it OK** to use quotations from Goethe?
> **Is it OK** to write in the margin?
> **Is it OK** if my dissertation is longer than 10,000 words?

> **Do you mind if** we go and work in the library?
> **Do you mind if** we miss the next seminar?

You could also see if something is allowed by using **Are we allowed to … ?** .

> **Are we allowed to** work in pairs?
> **Are we allowed to** retake the exam if we fail?

Saying what you like, dislike, prefer

The simplest way to talk about things you like is to use **I like …** . To talk about activities that you like doing, use **I enjoy …** .

> **I like** to read novels in the original language if I can.
> I quite **like** maths.

> **I enjoy** researching new topics.
> I really **enjoy** the practical work.

Useful words

a quotation	a sentence or phrase from a book, a poem, a speech or a play
the margin	the empty space down the side of a page
a dissertation	a long piece of writing on a subject you are studying
a seminar	a class at a college or university in which the teacher and a small group of students discuss a topic
a pair	two people who are doing something together
retake an exam	to take an exam again
a novel	a long written story about imaginary people and events
research	to study something and try to discover facts about it
practical	involving real situations and events rather than ideas and theories

> **GOOD TO KNOW!**
> **Like/Enjoy + -ing**
> When **like ...** or **enjoy ...** is followed by a verb, the verb is usually in the -ing form.

To tell someone what you do not like, use **I don't like ...** , or to make your view stronger, **I hate ...** .

> **I don't like** wasting time.
> **I don't like** physics.

> **I hate** being a student.
> I really **hate** working in the library.

A slightly formal way of saying what you don't like is **I dislike ...** .

> **I dislike** having to read aloud in class.
> **I dislike** the atmosphere in her class.
> **She disliked** the course's focus on painting.

If you want to say that you like one thing more than another, use **I prefer ...** . If you want to talk about the thing you like less, use **to** before it.

> **I prefer** history.
> **She prefers** using a computer.
> **I prefer** to study on my own.

Useful words
the atmosphere   the general feeling that you get when you are in a place
a focus   when you give special attention to something

To say that you would prefer to do something, use **I'd rather ...** . If you want to talk about the thing you like less, use **than**.

> **I'd rather** use the library **than** carry so many books around with me.
> **I'd rather** give up dance and concentrate on music.
> **We'd rather** take the exam next term.

Talking about your plans

If you have decided what you are going to do, you could use **I'm going to ...** or **I'm planning to ...** .

> **I'm going to** ask Dr Levy for some advice.
> **I'm going to** take a philosophy course this term.
> **I'm going to** finish my dissertation this week.

> **I'm planning to** stay at home tomorrow and revise.
> **I'm planning to** do a catering course.
> **I'm planning to** take a year off after school.

Useful words

concentrate on something	to give something all your attention
philosophy	the study of ideas about the meaning of life
a term	one of the periods of time that a school, college or university year is divided into
revise	to study something again in order to prepare for an exam
catering	providing food and drinks for people

If you are considering doing something, you could use **I'm thinking of ...** .

> **I'm thinking of** taking a gap year.
> **I'm thinking of** changing courses.
> **I'm thinking of** doing economics.

GOOD TO KNOW!
I'm thinking of + -ing
The verb that follows **I'm thinking of...** must be in the -ing form.

To talk about something that you would like to do but you are not sure if it is possible, use **I'm hoping to ...** .

> **I'm hoping to** go to university.
> **I'm hoping to** get a place at Oxford.
> **I'm hoping to** do business studies.

You can also use **I'm supposed to be ...** to show that there is some doubt about a plan.

> **I'm supposed to be** handing this in today.
> **I'm supposed to be** taking the exam in a month's time.
> **I'm supposed to be** doing a presentation to the class.

To ask someone about their plans, use **Are you going to ... ?** .

> **Are you going to** carry on with French?
> **Are you going to** work harder this term?
> **Are you going to** go to the library later?

Useful words

a gap year	a year between leaving school and starting university when you travel or work
a presentation	an occasion when someone shows or explains something to a group of people

● Listen out for

Here are some useful phrases you are likely to hear at school, college or university.

Turn to page 10.
Open your books at page 56.
Work in pairs/groups of 4.
Look it up in your dictionary.
Hand in your homework at the end of the lesson.
Make sure you read the questions carefully.
Put the equipment away when you have finished with it.
Make sure you check all your references.
Label your diagram.
Make sure your essay has a clear conclusion.
Write up the results of your experiments later today.
You must include a bibliography.

Useful words

look something up	to find a fact or piece of information by looking in a book or on a computer
a reference	a writer or a piece of work that you talk about in your writing
label	to write on something to explain what it is
a diagram	a simple drawing of lines
the conclusion	the part of an essay that shows your opinion about the subject
write up something	to write something using notes you made earlier
a bibliography	a list of the books you have used in your writing

Listen to the conversation: Track 25

Susie is talking to her tutor about what subjects to take next year.

A Could you give me some advice about what subjects to do next year? I really like art and I'd love to keep on with it, but some people say it takes up too much time, so I'm worried that it could be bad for my other subjects. I'm hoping to do politics and economics at university, so perhaps I should drop art?

B You're right that there's a lot of practical work for art. But in my opinion, if you love it enough, you'll find the time. But what about maths? If you're going to do economics, it might be a good idea to do that too.

A Are we allowed to do four subjects?

B Sure. Most of the bright students take four subjects. I'm sure you could manage it.

A I have a problem with maths – I just find it really difficult. I'd rather not do it if I don't have to.

B Oh. That could be a problem then. Is there a reason why you want to do economics? Why not do politics on its own, or with something else – a language for instance?

A That's a good idea. What's the best way to find out what courses are available?

B You need to make an appointment with the careers adviser – she'll help you.

A OK, I'll do that. Thanks for your help.

 Listen to more phrases and practise saying them: Track 26

Numbers, dates and time

Three, two, one... Go!

You will often need to use numbers in conversation. You will also need to talk about the time and dates. The phrases in this unit will help you to talk about all these things with confidence.

Numbers

To say how much something costs using the unit of money that is written as €, use **... euros** and to talk about the smaller unit used with the euro, use **... cents**. For the unit of money that is written as £, use **... pounds** and for the smaller unit used with the pound, use **... pence**.

> It cost me sixty-five **euros** twenty. (€65.20)
> That'll be eighteen **euros** and ninety-nine **cents**. (€18.99)
> At twenty-nine **dollars** each ($29), the price is very reasonable.
> He bought a bar of chocolate for eighty-nine **pence**. (89p)
> My ticket cost nine **pounds** fifty-nine. (£9.59)
> It was going to cost three hundred **pounds** (£300), which I couldn't afford.

To talk about how heavy something is using the units of measurement written as k and g, use **... kilos** and **... grams**. To talk about how heavy something is using the units of measurement written as lb and oz, use **... pounds** and **... ounces**.

> I'd like two **kilos** of potatoes, please.
> Can I have half a **kilo** of tomatoes?
> You need three **pounds** of apples.
> The recipe says two hundred **grams** of butter.

Useful words

reasonable	not too high
can afford something	to have enough money to pay for something
a recipe	a list of food and a set of instructions telling you how to cook something

To talk about how much liquid there is using the unit of measurement written as L or l, use **... litres**. For the unit of measurement written as p or pt, use **... pints**.

> I put twenty **litres** of petrol in the car yesterday.
> You need half a **litre** of milk for this recipe.
> Could you buy two **pints** of milk, please?

To talk about how long something is, using the units of measurement written as km, m and cm, use **... kilometres, ... metres** and **... centimetres**. For the units of measurement written as m, yd, ft and in, use **... miles, ... yards, ... feet** and **... inches**.

> We're thirty **kilometres** from Madrid.
> I'm one **metre** sixty-six **centimetres** tall.
> It's twenty **centimetres** long by ten wide.
> It's about eighty **miles** to Brighton.
> He's over six **feet** tall

To talk about amounts as parts of a hundred (%), use **... per cent**.

> Fifty-five **per cent** voted no.
> The rate of inflation is two point five **per cent**.
> Sixty-eight **per cent** of the population own their own homes.

For talking about a temperature, written as °, use **... degrees**.

> It's over thirty **degrees** in the shade today.
> It's only one or two **degrees** above zero.
> It's two or three **degrees** hotter today.

Useful words

vote	to show your choice officially at a meeting or in an election
a rate	how fast or how often something happens
inflation	a general increase in the prices of goods and services in a country
population	all the people who live in a country or an area
shade	an area where direct sunlight does not reach

To talk about the order in which something happens or comes, use **first, second, third,** etc ... .

> We're celebrating our **first** wedding anniversary today.
> This is my **second** trip to this region.
> He came **third** in the race.
> This is the **sixth** time I've eaten here.

The time

Use **... o'clock** to say what time it is when the clock shows the exact hour.

> He got up this morning at five **o'clock**.
> It's one **o'clock** – time for lunch!
> It's four **o'clock** in the afternoon.
> We're setting off at eight **o'clock** tomorrow morning.

> **GOOD TO KNOW!**
> **Midday** is used to mean twelve o'clock in the middle of the day.
> **Midnight** is used to mean twelve o'clock in the middle of the night.

To say that it is thirty minutes or less after a particular hour, use **... past ...** .

> It's twenty-five **past** one.
> It's five **past** six.
> It's quarter **past** one.
> She's coming here at half **past** five.

Useful words

celebrate	to do something enjoyable for a special reason
an anniversary	a date that is remembered because something special happened on that date in an earlier year
a trip	a journey that you make to a particular place and back again
a region	an area of the country or of the world
a race	a competition to see who is the fastest
set off	to start going somewhere

To say that it is a particular number of minutes before a particular hour, use **... to ...** .

> It's now twenty **to** one.
> It's ten **to** eight.
> I glanced at my watch and it was five **to** three.
> We landed in Cairo at quarter **to** one.

To find out the time now or the time that something starts, use **What time ... ?**.

> **What time** is it?
> Do you know **what time** it is?
> Could you tell me **what time** it is?
> **What time**'s the next train for Manchester?
> **What time** is the next performance?

To say the time that something is happening, use **at ...** .

> The lecture starts **at** seven o'clock.
> The train leaves **at** seven thirty.
> I'll see you **at** half past three.
> Let's meet up **at** quarter past five.

To say that something will happen at or before a particular time, use **by ...** .

> Can you be there **by** three o'clock?
> I have to leave **by** quarter to one.
> We have to finish this **by** quarter to two.

Useful words

glance	to look at someone or something very quickly
land	used for saying that an aeroplane comes down to the ground
a performance	when you entertain an audience by singing, dancing or acting
a lecture	a talk that someone gives in order to teach someone about a particular subject
meet up	to come together with someone, having planned to do this

● Listen out for

Here are some important phrases you may hear and use to do with the time.

Excuse me, do you have the time, please?
It's probably about eleven.
I'm in a hurry.
I must go – I'm late already.
We're running out of time.
Stop wasting time!
Did you get there on time?
How much time do we have left?
He should be here by now.

The train for Paris leaves at 13:55.
The 14:15 train to Strasbourg will depart from platform two.
Flight number 307 for London is due to take off at 20:45.
Flight 909 from Toronto is on time.

Saying how long

If you want to say that something will happen in so many minutes' time or in so many days' time, use **in ...** .

I'll be back **in** twenty minutes.
She'll be here **in** a week.
He completed the exercise **in** only three minutes.
I can probably do the job **in** an hour or two.

Useful words

in a hurry	needing or wanting to do something quickly
run out of something	to have no more of something left
waste	to use too much of something, such as time, doing something that is not important
on time	not late or early
due	expected to happen or arrive at a particular time
take off	used for saying that an aeroplane leaves the ground and starts flying
an exercise	an activity that you do in order to practise a skill

To ask how much time something lasts or how much time you need for something, use **How long ... ?**.

> **How long**'s the film?
> **How long** does the meeting usually last?
> **How long** will the tour take?

To say how much time is needed to do something, use **It takes ...** .

> **It takes** five minutes to make.
> **It took** two hours to reach the village.
> **It took** three hours by train.

The seasons

To say which season, (spring, summer, autumn or winter), something happens or happened in, use **in ...** .

> We get the best weather here **in** spring.
> We don't go camping **in** winter.
> They got married **in** the summer of 1999.
> They emigrated **in** the autumn of 1965.

To make it clear which spring, summer, etc. you are talking about, use **last ...** , **this ...** or **next ...** .

> I'm going to South Africa **this** winter.
> It was quite mild **last** winter.
> She's expecting her fifth baby **next** spring.

Useful words

a tour	a trip to an interesting place or around several interesting places
reach	to arrive at a place
camping	the activity of staying somewhere in a tent
get married	to legally become husband and wife in a special ceremony
emigrate	to leave your own country and go to live in another country
mild	not too cold
expect a baby	to have a baby growing inside you

The months of the year

To say which month of the year something happens or happened in, use **in ...** .

> The twins have their birthday **in** August.
> We'll probably go away on holiday **in** May.
> I visited some friends in Rome **in** September.
> We're going to the coast for our holidays **in** August.

To make it clear which January or February, etc. you are talking about, use
last ... , **this ...** or **next ...** .

> What are you doing **this** summer?
> Are you going abroad **this** summer?
> We went to Slovenia **last** June.
> I'm hoping to go to South America **next** July.

If you want to say which part of a month something happens in, use
at the start of ..., **in the middle of ...** or **at the end of ...** .

> She goes to university **at the start of** October.
> The summer holidays start **at the end of** June.
> They're moving **in the middle of** November.

Useful words

a twin	one of two people who were born at the same time to the same mother
the coast	the land that is next to the sea
abroad	in or to a foreign country
move	to go to live in a different place

Dates

To say what the date is, use **the first/second, etc. of March/November, etc.**
or **March/November, etc. the first/second, etc.**

> Its **the first of July** today.
> Tomorrow**'s the tenth of January**.
> It's **December the third** today.
> Next Monday will be **March the fifth**.

To say what date something is happening or happened on, use **on ...** before the date.

> He was born **on** the fourteenth of February, 1990.
> We got engaged **on** April the twenty-third.
> Barbara and Michael got married **on** May the fifteenth.
> Where do you think you'll be **on** the twentieth of October?

> **GOOD TO KNOW!**
> To ask what the date is, use **What's the date today?** .

The days of the week

To say what day of the week it is, use **It's ...** .

> 'What day is it today?' '**It's** Thursday.'
> **It's** Wednesday today, isn't it?
> Great! **It's** Saturday today.

When saying which day something happens or will happen, use **on ...** .

> I'm seeing the consultant **on** Thursday.
> It's my birthday **on** Tuesday.
> We'll see them **on** Wednesday.
> I don't work **on** Friday.

Useful words

get engaged	to agree to marry someone **a consultant** someone who gives expert advice on a subject
a consultant	someone who gives expert advice on a subject

To say what time of a particular day something happens, use **on … morning/afternoon/evening/night**.

> I'm going to see the estate agent **on Tuesday morning**.
> I'll see you **on Friday afternoon**.
> There was a good film on television **on Sunday evening**.
> What are you doing **on Saturday night**?

To say that you do something all Mondays/Saturdays, etc. use **every …** .

> We call her **every** Monday.
> He plays golf **every** Saturday.
> I used to see them **every** Friday.
> They go to the same café **every** Saturday morning.

To say that you do something one Wednesday/week, etc. and then not the next Wednesday/week, etc. and that it continues in this way, use **every other …** .

> He has the children **every other** weekend.
> We play football **every other** Saturday.
> Danielle and I have a coffee together **every other** Friday after work.
> **Every other** Sunday, we do a couple of hours' voluntary work.

To make it clear which Monday/Wednesday, etc. you are talking about, use **last … , this …** or **next …** .

> It's our wedding anniversary **this** Friday.
> I'm going on holiday **this** Tuesday.
> I had a job interview **last** Friday.
> Would **next** Friday be better for you?

Useful words

an estate agent	a person whose job is to sell buildings or land
a couple	two or around two people or things
voluntary	used for describing work that is done by people who are not paid, but who do it because they want to
an interview	a formal meeting in which someone asks you questions to find out if you are the right person for a job

numbers, dates and time

If you want to ask what day something is happening, use **What day ... ?**.

> **What day**'s the meeting? Is it Tuesday?
> **What day** is the bed being delivered?
> Do you know **what day** he's coming?
> I don't even know **what day** they're arriving.

To talk about a particular time the day after today, use **tomorrow ...** .

> I've got to be up early **tomorrow** morning.
> She leaves for Moscow **tomorrow** afternoon.
> I'm seeing her **tomorrow** evening.
> We're going to a party **tomorrow** night.

To talk about a particular time the day before today, use **yesterday ...** .

> It all happened **yesterday** morning while I was at work.
> He called at some point **yesterday** morning.
> I saw him in town **yesterday** afternoon.
> I heard my neighbours having a row **yesterday** evening.

> **GOOD TO KNOW!**
> To talk about the night that belonged to yesterday, you use **last night** and not **yesterday night**.

Useful words

deliver	to take something to a particular place
up	not in bed
a point	a particular time
a neighbour	someone who lives near you
a row	an argument

To say when something happened, use **...ago**.

> She called me a week **ago**.
> Gina and Alessandro left ten days **ago**.
> He was born three years **ago**.
> I have read his novel but it was ages **ago** now.

To say how long something has been happening, use **for ...**.

> It's been raining **for** five days
> I haven't seen them **for** three weeks.
> They haven't spoken to each other **for** months.
> She'd been waiting **for** over an hour and was a bit fed up.
> We've been living here **for** ten years now and we both feel it's time for a change.
> I haven't seen her **for** a week and I'm starting to feel a little concerned.

> **GOOD TO KNOW!**
> If you want to say 'for a long time' in conversation, use **for ages**.

Useful words

a novel	a long written story about imaginary people and events
ages	a long time
fed up	annoyed or bored
concerned	worried

● Listen out for

Here are some important phrases you may hear and use to do with dates, months of the year, days of the week and seasons.

When's your birthday?
It's my birthday today!
It's my parents' wedding anniversary today.
When are you getting married?
When are you going on holiday?
When do you start your course?
When are you going to New Zealand?
When do you come back from New Zealand?
When is the baby due?
When was Carlo born?
Which day do you play tennis on?
Which days of the week are you free?
Is Saturday any good for you?
How about this Saturday?
I'm afraid I'm busy on Saturday.
I'm afraid I can't make Saturday.
Which month is Lena's birthday in?
Which months are the hottest?
When is the rainy season?
When is the dry season?
They sometimes get snow during the winter months.
She spends the winter in Australia.

Useful words

good	suitable or convenient
make	to be present somewhere

Listen to the conversation: Track 27

Colleagues Brett and Emma are trying to arrange a time to meet.

A It would be good to get together and have a proper chat about this.

B Yes, I agree. Are you free to meet sometime this week?

A Possibly. Let me look in my diary. What about Wednesday morning?

B No, that's no good, I'm afraid. I'm in meetings on Wednesday morning. I could do Wednesday afternoon – before 3 o'clock. Is that any good for you?

A Well, I'm seeing a client for lunch in town on Wednesday. That should be finished by 2 o'clock. Mind you, it will take me half an hour to get back from town so that doesn't leave us much time.

B Okay, let's try another day. How about next Monday or Tuesday?

A So that's Monday 12th or Tuesday 13th. Let's see… yes, Monday morning looks good.

B Great. What time would you like to meet?

A How about 10:00?

B 10:00 sounds good. Shall I invite Ingrid? We met a couple of weeks ago to talk about the issue and I know she's very interested.

A Yes, good idea. Actually, I'm seeing her this afternoon so I'll mention it to her, if you like.

B Yes, please do.

A Okay, great. See you next Monday at 10:00.

B Yes, see you then.

 Listen to more phrases and practise saying them: Track 28

All the phrases by function ...

So, to sum up ...

This unit helps you find quickly all the phrases you have learned. You will find all the phrases that are used for the same function in one place under a heading.

Contents

Agreeing and disagreeing

To agree to do something or give someone something, use **Yes** or **OK**. To make **yes** more polite or enthusiastic, add **of course**.

> 'Will you come with me?' '**Yes**.'
> 'Could you help me with my bags?' '**Yes, of course**.'
> 'Can I have an ice cream, Dad?' '**Yes**.'
>
> 'Can you cook dinner tonight?' '**OK**, if you like.'
> 'Will you drive?' '**OK**.'
> 'Can I borrow your pen?' '**OK**.'

If you think that what someone has said is right, say **I agree ...** or **You're right**.

> **I agree**. I think she's great.
> Yes, **I agree** with you. We need to promote him.
>
> **You're right**. We waste too much food.
> I think **you're right** about the website.

If you feel strongly that what someone has said is right, say **I totally agree ...** .

> **I totally agree**. I think it's terrible.

To say you will not do something or give someone something, use **No**.

> 'Could you give me a lift?' '**No**, sorry, I haven't got time.'
> 'Will you pay for the ice creams?' '**No**, it's your turn.'

If you think that what someone has said is wrong, say **I disagree ...** and if you feel strongly that what someone has said is wrong, say **I totally disagree ...** .

> I'm afraid **I disagree**. I think it's a really bad idea.
>
> **I totally disagree**. I think it's a complete waste of money.

If you do not agree with someone's opinion, you can also use **I don't think so.** .

> 'Pierre's really nice, isn't he?' '**I don't think so.** He never speaks to me.'
> 'Travelling by train is really relaxing.' '**I don't think so.** I prefer to fly.'

Apologizing

To apologize, use I'm **sorry ...** or **Sorry ...** .

> **I'm sorry** you were late because of me.
> **I'm sorry** I missed your party.

> **Sorry** – I have to leave now.
> **Sorry**, I didn't hear what you were saying.

To make your apology stronger, use **I'm really sorry ...** or **I'm so sorry ...** .

> **I'm really sorry** I can't help you.

> **I'm so sorry** I upset you.

If you have to tell someone that there is a problem or that something bad has happened, start your sentence with **I'm afraid ...** .

> **I'm afraid** I can't come tonight.
> **I'm afraid** there's a problem with your order.

If someone says sorry to you, you can make them feel better by saying **It doesn't matter.** or **Don't worry about it.** .

> 'I'm sorry – I've spilled your drink.' '**It doesn't matter.**'
> 'Sorry we're late.' '**It doesn't matter** – I've only just got here myself.'

> 'Sorry I forgot your birthday.' '**Don't worry about it.**'
> 'I'm afraid the handle's come off the door.' '**Don't worry about it** – it happens all the time.'

A more informal way to tell someone that something does not matter is **No worries.** or **That's OK.** .

> 'Sorry I can't come to your party.' '**No worries**, I understand.'
> 'We've eaten all the food.' '**No worries**. I'm not hungry anyway.'

> 'Sorry about the noise.' '**That's OK** – it didn't bother me.'
> 'I didn't bring a coat.' '**That's OK** – I can lend you one.'

Asking for and giving explanations

The simplest way to ask for an explanation is to use **Why ... ?** .

> **Why** did you say that?
> **Why** don't you like Bella?
> **Why** do all living things die?

To ask for a reason, you can also use **What is the reason ... ?** .

> **What is the reason** for the change in temperature?
> **What was the reason** for Nelson Mandela's imprisonment?

Could you explain ... ? can also be used to ask someone to explain something, especially in a classroom.

> **Could you explain** how volcanos are formed?
> **Could you explain** why you came to this conclusion?

A slightly more informal way of asking for an explanation is **Why is it that ... ?** .

> **Why is it that** your hands can be cold while the rest of you is warm?
> **Why is it that** the glacier doesn't melt?

The simplest way of giving an explanation is to use **Because ...** .

> I was late **because** I missed the bus.
> **Because** heat cannot pass from a colder object to a warmer object.

You can also use **The reason is that ...** .

> **The reason is that** trees absorb the carbon dioxide.
> **The reason is that** the second number is larger than the first.

Asking for information

To ask for information, use the question words **Where ... ?**, **When ... ?**, **Why ... ?**, **Who ... ?**, **Which ... ?**, **What ... ?**, and **How ... ?**.

> **Where** is your office?

> **When** did you meet Olga?

Why did you leave Tokyo?

Who was there?

Which café was she in?

What's the name of the hotel?

How do I get his address?

To ask someone that you do not know for information you can use **Could you tell me ... ?** or **I'd like to know ...** . This makes the question slightly more polite.

Could you tell me where the train station is?
Could you tell me how much a ticket to Manchester is, please?

I'd like to know how much a double room would be.
I'd like to know whether you have any three-bedroom houses to rent.

Use **Tell me ...** to ask someone general questions about their life.

Tell me about your trip, Ian. Was it good?
Tell me about your work, Yuko. How's it going?

To ask someone to describe someone or something, use **What's ... like?**.

What's your hotel **like?**
What's his new girlfriend **like?** Is she nice?

To ask someone to describe a person's appearance, use **What does ... look like?**.

What does Jamie **look like?** Is he like his dad?
I don't know which one Pilar is. **What does** she **look like?**

We often use **Is ... ?** to start questions that require information.

Is he tall?
Is it far from the city centre?
Is breakfast included in the price?
Is she like her sister?
Is he a good teacher?

To ask questions about a particular thing, for example in a shop, use **Is this ... ?** or **Is it ... ?** .

> **Is this** the biggest size?
> **Are these** the only colours you have?
>
> **Is it** made of real leather?
> **Is it** big enough for four people?

To ask if a place has something, use **Is there ... ?**, or **Are there any ... ?** .

> **Is there** a hairdryer in the room?
> **Is there** much noise from the neighbours?
>
> **Are there any** good schools near here?
> **Are there any** more blankets in the room?

You could also use **Does ... have ... ?** to ask the same question.

> **Does** the flat **have** central heating?
> **Does** the hotel **have** a swimming pool?

To ask how to do something, use **How do you ... ?** .

> **How do you** get to the old town?
> **How do you** know which bus to catch?

To ask about time, use **What time ... ?** .

> **What time** does he get home?
> **What time** do we have to leave in the morning?

To ask about prices, use **How much ... ?** .

> **How much** rent do you pay?
> **How much** do you charge for breakfast?

To ask about the time that something took or will take, use **How long ... ?** .

> **How long** does the tour last?
> **How long** were you waiting?

How's ... ? is used to ask someone's opinion of the quality of something, or whether they are enjoying it.

> **How's** life in Madrid, Yewa? Are you enjoying it?
> **How was** the concert?

If you want someone who knows about something to suggest something that might be good or worth having, use **Can you recommend ... ?**.

> **Can you recommend** a hotel in the town centre?
> **Can you recommend** a good book for my holiday?

Use **Can you give me the number ... ?** to ask for the phone number of someone who can provide a service for you.

> **Can you give me the number** of a local dentist?
> **Can you give me the number** of a taxi service?

If you want to ask someone for advice about something, use **Could you give me some advice ... ?** . This phrase is followed by the prepositions **about** or **on**.

> **Could you give me some advice** on how to organise my essay?
> **Could you give me some advice** about English courses?

Asking for permission

To ask for permission, use **Can I ... ?**.

> **Can I** pay by credit card?
> **Can I** sit here?
> **Can we** camp here?

A more formal way of asking for permission is to use **May I ... ?**.

> **May I** borrow this guidebook?
> **May I** take this chair?
> **May I** use your phone, please?

To check if you can do something, use **Am I allowed to ... ?**.

> **Am I allowed to** use the washing machine?
> **Are we allowed to** ask questions?

If you want to check that someone will not be unhappy or angry if you do something, use **Do you mind if ... ?**.

> **Do you mind if** I park my car here for a moment?
> **Do you mind if** I leave my suitcase here for five minutes?
> **Do you mind if** I get there a bit later?

A slightly informal way of asking for permission is **Is it OK to ... ?**.

> **Is it OK to** try one of your oranges?
> **Is it OK to** take the alarm clock out of its box?
> **Is it OK to** leave our bags here?

Asking for things

To ask for something, use **Can I have ... ?**, **Could I have ... ?** or **I'd like ...** .
To be polite, use **please** at the beginning or end.

> **Can I have** two tickets for tonight's performance, please?
> **Can I have** an audio guide, please?

> **Could I have** a receipt, please?
> **Could we have** three seats together?

> **I'd like** a flat near the university.
> **I'd like** a map of the area, please.
> **I'd like** to stay three nights.

If it is important for you to have something, you can use **I need ...** .

> I urgently **need** her address.
> **We need** a guide who can speak English.

To describe the thing you want, use **I'm looking for ...** or **I want ...** .

> **I'm looking for** the coach station.
> **I'm looking for** a place to rent.

> **I want** a light summer jacket.
> **I want** to rent a house for six months.

If you want to ask if something you want is available, use **Do you have ... ?**, **Have you got ... ?**, or **Do you do ... ?**.

>   **Do you have** any brochures in English?
>   **Do you have** any tickets left for tomorrow's show?
>   **Do you have** any train timetables?

>   **Have you got** any strawberries?
>   **Have you got** a spare textbook?
>   **Have you got** a bag that I could have?

>   **Do you do** discounts for students?
>   **Do you do** this coat in any other sizes?
>   **Do you do** vegetarian meals?

To ask if a shop sells the thing you want, use **Do you sell ... ?**.

>   **Do you sell** light bulbs?
>   **Do you sell** newspapers?
>   **Do you sell** fresh bread?

When you have decided what you want to buy in a shop, use **I'll have ...** or **I'll take ...** .

>   **I'll have** a strawberry ice cream.
>   **I'll have** 200 grams of ham.

>   **I'll take** these two postcards.
>   **I'll take** the blue ones.

If you are asking someone if they can do something for you, use **Can you ... ?** or **Could you ... ?**. **Could you ... ?** is slightly more polite and formal than **Can you ... ?**.

>   **Can you** tell me what the opening hours are?
>   Please **can you** show me where we are on this map?

>   **Could you** call a taxi for me, please?
>   **Could you** get someone to repair the window?

A polite way of asking someone to do something is by saying **Would you mind ... ?**.

>   **Would you mind** translating this into English?
>   **Would you mind** giving me an estimate?

Would you mind emailing me the details, please?

To ask whether something you want is possible, use **Is it possible to ... ?**.

Is it possible to change these tickets for a later performance?
Is it possible to get an earlier appointment?
Is it possible to speak to the manager?

Attracting someone's attention

When you are asking for information you may need to get someone's attention before you can ask them a question. To do this, first say **excuse me**.

Excuse me, is the modern art museum near here?
Excuse me, do you know what time the gardens open?
Excuse me, where do I buy a ticket?

Complaining

To talk about something that is upsetting you, use **There's ...**, and for something you think is missing, use **There isn't ...** .

There's a leak in the ceiling.
There are mice under the floorboards.

There isn't any hot water.
There aren't any clean towels in the room.

If something is not good enough, use **I'm not happy with ...** or **I'm disappointed with ...** .

I'm not happy with the parking arrangements.
I'm not happy with my room.

I'm disappointed with the standard of the food.
I was disappointed with the service.

To say that you think something is bad, use **I think ...** .

I think the beds are really uncomfortable.
I don't think the rooms are cleaned often enough.

Congratulating someone

To show that you are pleased that something good has happened to someone, use **Congratulations!**.

> **Congratulations** on your new job!
> **Congratulations** on the birth of your baby son!
> You passed your exam? **Congratulations!**

To show that you think someone has done something very well, use **Well done!**.

> **Well done**, Mercedes!
> 'I got that job, by the way.' **'Well done!** That's great!'
> 'Look, I've tidied up all those papers.' **'Well done!'**

Dangers and emergencies

To ask for help because you are in danger, shout **Help!**.

> **Help!** I can't swim!
> **Help!** The building's on fire!

To tell someone that they are in danger, shout **Look out!**.

> **Look out!** There's a car coming!
> **Look out!** It's falling!

To tell someone to pay attention so that they do not have an accident, use **Be careful ...**.

> **Be careful** on those steps!
> **Be careful!** It's icy outside.
> **Be careful** with those scissors!

Describing people and things

Start general descriptions of things with **It's ...** and of people with **He's/She's ...**.

> **It's** gold with three diamonds.
> **It's** a ladies' watch.
> **It's** a green suitcase with wheels.

He's five years old.
She's Spanish.
He was very tall.

Use **It's made of ...** to say what material or substance something is.

It's made of leather.
It's quite a small bag, and **it's made of** velvet.
The beads are bright blue and **they're made of** glass.

Use **He's/She's got ...** to talk about what someone looks like.

She's got short blond hair.
He's got a beard.
She's got a big nose.

To talk about someone's clothes, use **He's/She's wearing ...** .

She's wearing jeans and a green T-shirt.
She's wearing an orange blouse.
He's wearing a black jacket.

Encouraging someone

To encourage someone to go somewhere more quickly or to do something more quickly, use **Hurry up!** .

Hurry up! We've got to be there in ten minutes!
Hurry up! We're late already!
Hurry up, Mario! When you've finished your work, you can go out to play.

To encourage someone to go somewhere or to do something more quickly, you can also use **Come on!** .

Come on, Helena, or we'll be late!
Come on! We're going to miss our train!
Come on! We haven't got all day!
Come on! Have a swim with us. The water's lovely!

To encourage someone to do something, you can use **Go for it!** . **Go for it!** is slightly informal.

> 'I'm thinking of applying for that job.' **'Go for it!'**
> 'I've decided I want to run a marathon.' **'Go for it!'**
> 'I'd like to go and see Paolo in New York.' **'Go for it!'**

Explaining a problem

To explain a general problem, use **I've got a problem ...** . Use the preposition **with** to talk about a thing that is causing your problem.

> **I've got a problem** – this homework has to be done by tomorrow, but I haven't got the books I need.
> **I've got a problem with** my essay – it's far too long and I don't know what to cut out.
> **We've got a problem with** our central heating.

If you are asking somebody for help, you will need to be able to describe the problem. Use **There's ...** to say what the problem is.

> **There's** a smell of gas in my room.
> **There's** a noise coming from the engine.
> **There are** mice in the kitchen.

If the problem is that you do not have something you need, use **There isn't ...** or **I haven't got ...** .

> **There isn't** any soap in the bathroom.
> **There isn't** enough food for everyone.
> **There aren't** any towels in my room.

> **I haven't got** her address.
> **She hasn't got** enough money.
> **He hasn't got** a car.

For some problems, you can use **I've got ...** .

> **I've got** a problem.
> **I've got** a flat tyre.
> **I've got** too much work.

If the problem is that you are not able to do something, use **I can't ...** .

> **I can't** drive.
> **We can't** open the bedroom door.
> **I can't** find my keys.

If you want to say that you do not understand something, use **I don't understand ...** .

> **I don't understand** what he's saying.
> **I don't understand** the instructions.
> **I don't understand** how to use this phone.

If you do not have the knowledge to do something, use **I don't know how to ...** .

> **I don't know how to** get my email.
> **We don't know how to** get there.
> **I don't know how to** change a fuse.

If a piece of equipment will not do what you want it to do, use **The ... won't ...** .

> **The** engine **won't** start.
> **The** barbecue **won't** light.
> **The** shower **won't** work.

Expressing opinions

If you want to give your opinion about something, use **I think ...** .

> **I think** their website is excellent.
> **I thought** he was very reasonable.
> **I don't think** they did a very good job.

You can also give your opinion of something by saying **in my opinion ...** .

> **In my opinion**, these targets are too high.
> **In my opinion**, she's in the wrong job.

To ask someone for their opinion, say **What do you think of ... ?**.

> **What do you think of** her abilities?
> **What did you think of** the meal?

You can also ask someone for their opinion by saying **What's your opinion of ... ?**.

> **What's your opinion of** the company?
> **What's your opinion of** their performance?

To ask someone if they think something is a good idea, use **What do you think about ... ?** .

> **What do you think about** going out for dinner tonight?
> **What do you think about** inviting Eva?
> **What do you think about** going to France this year for our holidays?

Expressing surprise

A simple way to show that you are surprised by what someone has said is to use **Really?** .

> 'Zareb is leaving?' '**Really?** Why?'
> 'I don't think it's a very good school.' '**Really?** I was very impressed by it.'
> 'I'm terrible at maths?' '**Really?** I can't believe that!'

A stronger way to show that you are surprised by what someone has said is to say **That's incredible!** or **That's amazing!** .

> You ran twenty miles in two and a half hours? **That's incredible!**
> So Steve works a sixty-hour week? **That's incredible!**

> Camille spent two thousand pounds on a jacket? **That's amazing!**
> You cooked for sixty people? **That's amazing!**

An informal way to show surprise at what someone has said is to say **You're kidding!** .

> 'Daniel is leaving.' '**You're kidding!** He's only been in the job three months!'
> 'They're buying a house in Bath.' '**You're kidding!** Another house?'

Expressing sympathy

The most common way to show that you are sad for someone when something bad has happened is to use **I'm (so) sorry.** or **I'm sorry to hear ...** .

> Diana told me about your brother's accident. **I'm so sorry.**

I heard that Charlie had lost his job, Sara. **I'm sorry.**

I'm so sorry to hear that your mother died.
I was very sorry to hear that Julia and Marco had split up.

To show that you are sorry when something slightly bad or disappointing has happened, use **It's a shame ...** or **It's a pity ...** .

It's a shame you couldn't come with us last night.
It's a shame she didn't pass her exam after all that hard work.

It's a pity you can't stay longer.
It's a pity your mother won't be there.

Hellos and goodbyes

Use **Hello ...** as a general greeting. It is polite to say **hello** to anyone in any situation.

Hello Jorge.
Hello Dr Ahmed.

Use **Hi ...** in informal situations, for example when you are meeting friends.

Hi, how are things with you?
Hi, how are you doing?
Oh **hi** Adam, I didn't know you were coming.

Use **Good morning, Good afternoon** or **Good evening** in slightly more formal situations, for instance if you meet a neighbour, or when you see people at work.

Good morning everyone. Today we are going to be looking at how to form questions.
Good afternoon Mr Kowalski.

Use **Goodbye ...** when you leave someone.

Goodbye Clara, have a safe journey.

Goodbye ... is often shortened to **Bye ...** .

Bye everyone!

Use **Goodnight ...** when you are going to bed, or if someone else is going to bed.

> **Goodnight** everyone – see you in the morning.

See you ... is a slightly informal way of saying goodbye to someone you know you will see again.

> OK, I need to go now. **See you!**
> **See you** tomorrow!
> **See you** on Monday!

If someone has come to a place for the first time, you can use **Welcome!** .

> **Welcome!** I'm so pleased you could come.
> **Welcome** to the UK!
> **Welcome** to Cambridge!

Introducing people

If you want to introduce someone to someone else, use **This is ...** .

> **This is** my husband, Richard.
> **This is** Medina, my friend from school.
> **These are** my children, Theo, Ruby and Phoebe.

In slightly formal situations, use **I'd like you to meet ...** or **Can I introduce you to ... ?**.

> **I'd like you to meet** Dr Bjornson. Dr Bjornson has been working on our project.
> **I'd like you to meet** our head of department, Anke Hub.

> **Can I introduce you to** my husband, Andre?
> **Can I introduce you to** Otto, who's going to be giving a talk later?

> **GOOD TO KNOW!**
> When you are introduced to someone, you can just say **Hello**, or in a slightly more formal situation, say **Pleased to meet you**.

Making arrangements

When you make arrangements with someone, you may want to check if they are happy with them. Use **Would it suit you ... ?**.

> **Would it suit you** to meet a little earlier?
> **Would it suit you** if I met you at the restaurant?
> **Would it suit you** better if we went by train?

To ask someone if they would prefer a different arrangement, use **Would you prefer it if ... ?** or **Would it be better ... ?**.

> **Would you prefer it if** we didn't invite Claudia?
> **Would you prefer it if** we came to see you the next weekend?

> **Would it be better** to cycle there?
> **Would it be better** if we ate out somewhere?
> **Would it be better** if we took some food with us?

To make sure someone is happy with a plan, use **Is ... OK?**.

> **Is** seven o'clock for dinner **OK** or is that too early for you?
> I was thinking of the Greek restaurant on Southbourne Street. **Is** that **OK** with you?
> **Is** it **OK** if I don't come?
> **Is** it **OK** to meet after the film?

Another way to make sure that someone is happy with a plan is to use **How does ... sound?**.

> I was thinking we'd meet for dinner and the see a film. **How does** that **sound**?
> What about a week in France followed by a week in Spain? **How does** that **sound**?
> What about a coffee in The Book Shop café, followed by shopping. **How does** that **sound**?
> **How does** eight-thirty for dinner **sound**?

A common way to agree on the time or date of arrangement is to use **Shall we say ... ?**.

> So what time are we meeting? **Shall we say** eight o'clock – or is that too late?

Lunch at Café Otto sounds cool. **Shall we say** one o'clock inside the café?
Shall we say twelve-thirty in the book shop? Is that okay?
Shall we say seven o'clock for dinner? Does that suit you?

Making suggestions

One easy way of making a suggestion is to use **We could ...** .

We could go and see a film.
We could call Rav and see what he says.
We could go for a walk, if you like.

> **GOOD TO KNOW!**
> When people start a sentence with **We could ...** they often add **if you like** at the end.

If you are eager to do something with someone, use **Let's ...** .

Let's have a party!
Let's buy tickets for Saturday's match.
I've got a good idea. **Let's** all go swimming.

Another way to make a suggestion is to use **Shall we ... ?**.

Shall we go out for dinner?
Shall we have a barbecue and invite some friends round?
Shall we get her a present?

If you have an idea, use **How about ... ?** or **What about ... ?**.

How about going somewhere for a coffee?
How about going bowling?

What about asking Tahir to join us?
What about taking a picnic to the park?

> **GOOD TO KNOW!**
> **How about/What about + -ing**
> A verb that comes after **How about ... ?** or **What about ... ?** must be in the -ing form.

To suggest what someone else can do or where someone else can go, use
You could ... .

> **You could** rent an apartment for a while.
> After your meal, **you could** have ice-creams on the terrace.

You can also use **Why not ... ?** or **Why don't ... ?** if you have an idea about what
someone else might do.

> **Why not** ask Melissa to help out?
> If you don't have anything to do, **why not** go to Helena's party?

> **Why don't** we buy a tent?
> **Why don't** you come along to the party after the film?

I suggest ... and **You should ...** are slightly strong ways of making a suggestion.

> **I suggest** we get a taxi there.

> **You should** look online and see if you can get something cheaper.

Making sure you've understood

If you do not understand what someone has said, use **I don't understand.** .

> Sorry, **I don't understand**.
> **I don't understand** what you said.
> Please could you repeat that? **I didn't understand**.

You can ask for help with understanding by using **Would you mind ... ?** .

> **Would you mind** speaking more slowly?
> **Would you mind** repeating that?
> **Would you mind** speaking in English?

To check the meaning of a word, use **What does ... mean?** .

> **What does** 'fragile' **mean**?
> **What does** 'end up' **mean**?
> **What does** 'out of order' **mean**?

> **GOOD TO KNOW!**
> If you do not hear what someone has said and you want them to repeat it, use **Pardon?** or **Sorry?**.

Please and thank you

When asking for something from someone, use **please**.

> Two kilos of oranges, **please**.
> A large apple tart, **please**.
> Could you give these to Anders, **please**?
> **Please** could I borrow this chair?
> **Please** could you tidy up now?

To say that you would like something that someone has offered you, use **Yes, please.** .

> 'Would you like some more coffee?' '**Yes, please**.'
> 'Do you need a bag?' '**Yes, please**.'
> 'Can I help you with those bags?' 'Oh, **yes, please**.'
> 'Would you like me to post this for you?' '**Yes, please**.'

To thank someone, use **Thank you** or **Thanks**. **Thanks** is slightly informal.

> **Thank you** for all your help, Zalika.
> **Thank you** very much for coming here tonight.
> 'Here's a little birthday present.' '**Thank you!**'
> 'You look lovely in that dress.' '**Thank you**, Judy.'

> **GOOD TO KNOW!**
> To make **Thank you** or **Thanks** stronger, use **very much** after it.

> 'Here, have a cup of coffee.' '**Thanks**, Roman.'
> 'I love your new haircut.' '**Thanks**, Juliana.'
> Hey, **thanks** for helping out at the weekend, Anneli. I really appreciate it.
> **Thanks** very much for all those books you gave us for the children. It was very kind of you.

> **GOOD TO KNOW!**
> People often say something extra after saying **thank you** or **thanks** to make it stronger. For example they often say **I appreciate it** or **It was a great help**. They also sometimes say **It was very kind of you**.

To accept someone's thanks, use **You're welcome.** or **Not at all.** .

> 'Thank you very much for all your help, John. We do appreciate it.'
> '**You're welcome.**'
> 'Thanks for dinner last night. It was really lovely.' '**You're welcome.**
> Any time.'

> 'Thanks for looking after the children on Saturday – that was a great
> help, Lucia.' '**Not at all.**'
> 'Thank you for lending me the book. I loved it.' '**Not at all.**'

Another way of accepting someone's thanks is to use **It's my pleasure.** or
My pleasure. This is a slightly more formal way of accepting thanks.

> 'Thank you for the lovely gifts.' '**It's my pleasure.**'
> 'Thank you very much for your cheque, Charlotte. It was very kind of you.'
> '**It's my pleasure.**'

> 'Thank you, Simone.' '**My pleasure.**'
> 'Thank you, Ben – you've been a great help.' '**My pleasure.**'

To accept thanks from a person that you know, use **That's all right.** .

> 'Thanks for your help, mate.' '**That's all right.**'
> 'A present for me? Thanks, Patrick.' '**That's all right.**'

Another way of accepting thanks from a person that you know is to use
No problem. .

> 'Thanks for looking after Rosie – it was a great help.' '**No problem.**'
> 'Thanks for the party invitation.' '**No problem.**'

Saying what you have to do

To tell someone that it is very important that you do something, use **I have to
...** or **I need to ...** .

> **I have to** call my mother.
> I really **have to** finish this piece of work today.
> **You** don't **have to** work till eight o'clock every evening.

I **need to** get some money out.
I **need to** cancel that order.
We **need to** book our flights.

To ask what someone has to do, use **Do you have to ... ?** .

Do you have to pay for the work yourself?
Do you have to tell them?

Another way of saying that it is important that you do something is **I must ...** .
This is used especially when it is *very* important that you do something.

I **must** let Vincenzo know.
We **must** find someone else to do the work.

If something is important, you could use **It is important for me to ...** .

It is important for me to pass this exam.
It is important for me to work as hard as possible.

Use **I should ...** or **I ought to ...** to say what is the right thing to do, even if you
are not going to do it.

I **should** call Sergei and let him know.
I really **should** go to the gym.
We really **should** invite both sets of parents.

I **ought to** take that radio back.
I **ought to** invite Sandro.
We **ought to** pay Walkers for the work they've done.

> **GOOD TO KNOW!**
> There is no 'to' after **I should ...** .

Saying what you like, dislike, prefer

The simplest way to say that you like something is to use **I like ...** . To say that
you like doing an activity, use **I enjoy ...** . To ask someone if they like or enjoy
something, use **Do you like ... ?** or **Do you enjoy ... ?**.

I like dancing.
Do you like driving?

I **enjoy** just looking out of the window.
Do you enjoy exploring new places?

If you like something, but not in a strong way, use **I quite like ...** .

I **quite like** going to films.
I **quite like** the ballet.
I **quite like** exploring new places.

If you want to say that you like something very much, use **I really like ...** or
I love ... .

I **really like** Italian food.
I **really like** travelling because you get to see a different way of life.
I **really like** looking around cities.

I **love** looking at the scenery from the train.
I **love** eating out.
I **love** meeting new people.

To say that you do not like something, use **I don't like ...** , or to say that you
really do not like something, use **I hate ...** .

I **don't like** flying.
He doesn't like shopping.
They don't like fish.

I **hate** getting stuck in traffic.
I **hate** long-haul flights.
I **hate** winter in this country.

You can also use **I can't bear ...** to say that you *really* do not like something.

I **can't bear** crowded shops.
I **can't bear** the heat.

If you want to say that you like one thing more than another thing, use
I prefer ... . To talk about the thing that you like less, use **to** before it.

I **prefer** going on the train **to** driving.
I do travel on my own but I **prefer** travelling with other people.

Saying what you want to do

To talk about what you would like to do, use **I'd like to ...** or **I want to ...** .

> **I'd like to** get home early tonight.
> **I'd like to** meet your brother.
>
> **I want to** leave by 5 this afternoon.
> **I want to** speak to her as soon as possible.

If you are very eager to do something, use **I'd really like to ...** or **I'd love to ...** .

> **I'd really like to** see the Great Wall of China.
> **I'd really like to** take the children to the beach.
>
> **I'd love to** go to the cinema.
> **I'd love to** go walking in the mountains.

A slightly informal way of saying what you would like to do or have is **I (quite) fancy ...** or **I wouldn't mind ...** .

> **I fancy** going to a disco.
> **I quite fancy** a swim.
>
> **I wouldn't mind** going to see a film.
> **I wouldn't mind** something to eat.

You can also use **I'm quite keen to ...** to say that you would like to do something.

> **I'm quite keen to** get home early tonight as I have to be up early tomorrow morning.
> **I'm quite keen to** get this bit of work done.

Use **I'd prefer to ...** or **I'd rather ...** when you want to do one thing and not another.

> **I'd prefer to** go to a local hospital.
> **I'd prefer to** see a female doctor.
>
> **I'd rather** have the operation next week.
> **I'd rather** spend a bit more and get a better place.

Use **Would you prefer to ... ?** or **Would you rather ... ?** to ask someone if they would like to do one thing and not another.

> **Would you prefer to** stay in tonight?
> **Would you prefer to** spend a bit less?

> **Would you rather** eat a bit earlier?
> **Would you rather** spend more time with the children?

Talking about your health

After saying hello to someone, especially someone we know, we usually ask about their health, by saying **How are you?** .

> Hello, Jan. **How are you?**
> It's great to see you, Anna. **How are you?**

> **GOOD TO KNOW!**
> To answer that question, use **I'm fine, thanks.** or **I'm good thanks.** .
> If you are not well, you could say **Not great, really.** or **Not too good, actually.** .

If you need to describe a medical problem, you can use **I've got ...** .

> **I've got** a temperature.
> **I've got** a cold.
> **I've got** asthma.

If you want to say which part of your body hurts, use **my ... hurts**.

> **My** back **hurts**.
> **His** foot **hurts**.
> **My** neck **hurts**.

If the pain you have is an ache, you can say which part of your body it is in by using **I've got ... ache**.

> **I've got** a head**ache**.
> **I've got** stomach **ache**.
> **She's got** tooth**ache**.

You can talk about more general problems that you are having using **I feel ...** .

> **I feel** tired all the time.
> **I feel** sick.
> **I feel** better now.

Talking about your plans

Use **I'm + -ing verb ...** or **I'm going to ...** to talk about plans that you are sure of.

> **I'm spending** a couple of days with my parents.
> **They're going** on a package holiday this summer, as usual.
> **I'm having** a stopover in Thailand on the way there.

> **I'm going to** do a course in London.
> **I'm going to** travel first-class.
> **I'm going to** take the kids to the park.

Use **Are you going to ... ?** or **Will you ... ?** to ask someone about their plans.

> **Are you going to** travel with Tahir?
> **Are you going to** tell Alex?
> **Are you going to** see Sophia while you're in Milan?

> **Will you** manage to do any sightseeing in between meetings?
> **Will you** charge us extra for the bigger room?
> **Will you** call me when you get home?

To talk about your plans, you can also use **I'm planning to ...** or, if you are slightly less sure, **I'm hoping to ...** .

> **I'm planning to** spend a few days in Berlin.
> **We're planning to** drive along the coast.
> **Jack and Millie are planning to** come over this year.

> **I'm hoping to** stay in youth hostels most of the time.
> **She's hoping to** do a tour of the nearby islands.
> **We're hoping to** fit in some skiing while we're in the mountains.

To talk about a plan that is only possible, use **I might ...** .

> **I might** book a hotel for that night.
> **I might** spend an extra week in Calgary.
> **I might** stay on if I like it there.

To talk about something that should happen in the future, use **I'm supposed to ...** .

> **I'm supposed to** be at the station by 8:00.
> **I'm supposed to** be meeting Brett in Paris.
> What time **are we supposed to** get there?
> **He's supposed to** be driving me to the airport.

Talking about yourself

To say what your name is, use **I'm ...** or, in a slightly more formal situation, **My name's ...** .

> Hi, **I'm** Tariq – I'm a friend of Susie.
> **I'm** Paul – I'm your teacher for this week.

> **My name's** Johann.
> **My name's** Yuko – I'm Kazuo's sister.

To give general information about yourself, use **I'm ...** .

> **I'm** a friend of Paolo's.
> **I'm** married with two children.
> **I'm** training for the London Marathon.

You can also give general information about yourself using **I've got ...** .

> **I've got** some friends who live in Nairobi.
> **I've got** relatives in Australia.
> **We've got** a cottage in France.

To talk about your work, use **I'm ...** with the name of a job, or **I work ...** to say something more general about what you do.

> **I'm** a doctor.
> **I'm** a bus driver.

I **work** for an oil company.
I **work** as a translator.

> **GOOD TO KNOW!**
> If you want to ask someone what their job is, use **What do you do?**.

To talk about where you live, use **I live ...** or **I'm from ...** . **I'm from ...** is also used to talk about where you were born and lived as a child, even if you do not live there now.

I **live** in Wales.
We live near Moscow.

I'm from Poland originally, but I live in Paris now.
We're from Manchester.
My family's from India – my parents moved here in 1970.

> **GOOD TO KNOW!**
> To ask someone where they live, use **Where do you live?** or **Where are you from?**.

A more formal way of saying where you live is to use **my address is ...** .

My address is 29 Kelvin Close, L3 0QT Liverpool.
My address in England **is** 6 Green Street, Wellington.
My permanent **address is** 7 avenue Foch in Aix.

If you are in a place for a short time, either on holiday or for work, you can say where you are living by using **I'm staying ...** .

I'm staying at the Hotel Tulip.
I'm staying with friends in Budapest.
I'm staying in Paris for a week.

Grammar

Verb tenses

The present simple

The present simple tense is used for things that happen regularly or things that are always true.

> They often **go** to the cinema on Saturdays.
> He **watches** a lot of TV.
> I don't **like** coffee.
> The sun **rises** in the east.

It is also used to show the speaker's opinions or beliefs.

> I **think** he's a very good teacher.
> I **don't agree** with that at all.

We also use the present simple for planned future actions with a time adverb, for example to talk about travel plans.

> The train **leaves** at 10.40 a.m.
> Our plan **lands** at 6.30.

The present continuous

We use the present continuous to talk about things that are happening now, at the time when we are talking.

> I can't come out – I'm **doing** my homework.
> He's **cooking** the dinner.

The present continuous is also used for talking about temporary situations.

> She's **staying** with friends at the moment.
> He's **working** with Frieda this week.

We also use the present continuous to talk about arrangements for future events.

> I'm **flying** to New York next week.
> I'm **seeing** Milos tonight.

The past simple

The past simple tense is used for single actions in the past.

> I **met** Charlotte in the café.
> We **walked** around the park.

It is also used for repeated actions in the past, often with *always*, *never* or *often*.

> I often **had** lunch with her.
> We always **sent** each other birthday cards.

The present perfect

The present perfect is used to talk about things that happened or were done and completed in the past, but which have some connection with the present. When you use the present perfect, you do not mention a specific time.

> Her daughter **has had** an accident.
> They **have bought** their tickets.
> **Have** you **bought** your tickets yet?

The present perfect is often used to answer the question *How long … ?* together with *for* to talk about a period of time, or *since* to talk about the length of time from a particular point.

> How long **have** you **lived** in Edinburgh?
> I **have lived** in Edinburgh for fifteen years.
> We**'ve had** this car since 2009
> We **haven't spoken** to each other since the night of the argument.

The past continuous

The past continuous is used to talk about things that began in the past but were not finished, or that were interrupted. It is often used with specific times.

> What **were** you **doing** at eight o'clock last night?
> I **was waiting** for a bus.
> We **were sitting** in the kitchen when Dad came in.

It is also used to describe a scene in the past, especially in a story.

> It was a dreadful morning – the snow **was** still **falling** and the wind
>   **was howling** round the house.
> The trees **were beginning** to lose their leaves.

The past perfect

The past perfect is used to talk about things that happened in the past before
something else happened or before a particular time.

> **Had** you ever **seen** her before then?
> No, I **hadn't seen** her.
> She **had** just **made** some coffee when I arrived.

It is often used with a time expression such as *always* or *for several days*.

> We **had** always **wanted** to visit Canada, so last year we decided to go.
> It **had rained** continuously for several days.

The future simple

The future simple is used to talk about things in the future.

> I **will come** and see you tomorrow.
> She**'ll** phone you later.
> They**'ll** eat at the restaurant.

Modal verbs

Modal verbs are verbs such as **might**, **could** and **will**. They express ideas such as
possibility, permission or necessity.

These are the modal verbs, with their negative forms and short forms.

Modal verb	Negative	Negative short form
can	cannot	can't
could	could not	couldn't
may	may not	—
might	might not	mightn't
must	must not	mustn't

shall	shall not	shan't
will	will not	won't
should	should not	shouldn't
would	would not	wouldn't
ought to	ought not to	oughtn't to

Can you see the lions?
I **couldn't** find my keys.
I **may** see Joe tomorrow.
They said they **might** be late.
I **mustn't** forget to phone David.
Shall we take a taxi?
Will Lorna be there?
You **shouldn't** work so hard.
Would you like an apple?
I **ought to** take more exercise.

We also use **need** and **have to** as modal verbs.

I **needn't** get any more food.
He **has to** go to London.

How modal verbs behave

Modal verbs behave in a different way from other verbs.

The form of modal verbs does not change. So, for instance, if you use a modal verb with he/she/it, it does *not* add an 's'.

She may be home late.
It should work better now.

They cannot be used as a main verb on their own – they must always be followed by another verb. There is no 'to' infinitive form for modal verbs. If there is no auxiliary verb (be or have) before the main verb, the main verb must be in the base (infinitive) form. Remember not to use 'to' before it.

Yes, you **can borrow** those earrings tonight.
You **should try** that new restaurant in town.
You **must come** over again some time.
I **may decide** to change my job.

If one of the auxiliary verbs **have** or **be** follows the modal verb, the main verb will be in the appropriate present or past participle form.

> I **may have upset** him.
> You **could have looked** for it yourself.
> Janice **might be coming** too.
> Sue **should be** happy about this.

Making negatives with modal verbs

To make a negative, put the word **not** *after* the modal and *before* the following verb. Remember not to use 'to' before the verb.

> You **must not forget** to phone her.
> They **will not leave** their house.

Modal negatives often use short forms, especially in speech and informal writing.

> He **won't give** me the money he owes me.
> We **couldn't see** the screen.

Making past tenses with modal verbs

Modal verbs only have one tense, the present simple. The present perfect tense is shown by the form of the verb that comes after the modal verb.

> They **might not have seen** the letter.
> I **would have asked** her if I'd known.
> They **should have arrived** earlier.
> He **ought to have had** more sense.

However, one of the meanings of **could** is as a past tense of **can**, and one of the meanings of **would** is as a past tense of **will**.

> I **could see** them coming.
> They **couldn't find** the book.
> He **wouldn't tell** us what happened.
> The car **wouldn't start**.

The modal verb **must** is expressed by **had to** in the past.

> I **must finish** my work.
> I **had to finish** my work.
> They **must pay** for the damage.
> They **had to pay** for the damage.

The uses of modal verbs

Modal verbs are used to add particular kinds of meaning. These are some of the main ones.

To express doubt or possibility.

> I **may not be able** to do it.
> I think I **might have caught** your cold.

To express degrees of future possibility.

> I **may be** late home tomorrow evening.
> You **will be seeing** her on Friday at Jackie's house.

To ask for or give permission.

> **May** I **come in**?
> You **can borrow** my car if you like.

To say that someone is not allowed to do something. This meaning uses **not** or a short form **–n't** after the modal verb.

> You **shouldn't use** this computer without permission.
> He **must not see** this letter.

To say what you think might happen or be true.

> The weather's so bad the flight **could be** late.
> It **might be** all over by the time we get there.

To give intructions or advice.

> I **must give in** my essay today.
> Helen **ought to tell** the truth.

To ask people to do something.

> **Would** you please **close** the door?
> **Could** you **get** me a pen?

Short forms

In English, we often use short forms of words, for example **I'm** (I am), **he'll** (he will), **didn't** (did not). In conversation we almost always use these forms – it would sound strange to say the words in their full form. These forms can also be used in informal writing.

We use an apostrophe (') to represent the missing letters.

These are the short forms we use.
> **'m** = am
> **'s** = is *or* has
> **'re** = are
> **'ve** = have
> **'ll** = will
> **'d** = would *or* had

> **I'm** very happy.
> **They're** having a party.
> **We've** finished our work.
> **He'll** ring you later.

's can mean either **is** or **has**.

> **Mum's** busy at the moment. (= Mum is)
> **He's** in the garden. (= he is)
> **She's** seen it before. (= she has)
> **Who's** eaten the cake? (= who has)

'd can mean either **would** or **had**.

> **I'd** like a cup of tea. (= I would)
> He said **he'd** do it later. (= he would)
> **She'd** gone to the shops. (= she had)
> **They'd** lost their dog. (= they had)

Another common contracted form is **Let's**, which means **let us**. We never use the full form for this – it sounds very old-fashioned and formal.

> **Let's** to to the beach.
> **Let's** see what Martina says.

Short forms in negatives

Short forms are also used for negatives made with the auxiliary verbs be, have and do, and with modal verbs such as can, will and must.

These are the negative short forms made with auxiliary verbs.

be	have	do
isn't = is not	**haven't** = have not	**don't** = do not
aren't = are not	**hasn't** = has not	**doesn't** = does not
wasn't = was not	**hadn't** = had not	**didn't** = did not
weren't = were not		

> My house **isn't** far from here.
> We **weren't** doing anything wrong.
> I **haven't** been to America.
> She **hasn't** seen the movie.
> I **don't** know anything about it.
> They **didn't** like the food.

These are negative short forms made with modal verbs.

can't = cannot	**wouldn't** = would not	**shan't** = shall not
couldn't = could not	**mustn't** = must not	**needn't** = need not
won't = will not	**shouldn't** = should not	**oughtn't** = ought not

You **can't** go inside the building.
We **couldn't** find him.
It **won't** rain today.
She **wouldn't** help us.
You **needn't** do the washing up.
I **shouldn't** eat so much.

Countable and uncountable nouns

Countable nouns are the words for things that we can count. They have singular and plural forms. They can have **a** or **an** in front of them. If they are singular, they *must* have a word like **a**, **an**, **the** or **his** in front of them.

She ate **an apple**.
Where shall I put **my coat**?

Uncountable nouns are the words for things that cannot be counted. They cannot have **a** or **an** in front of them, and they do not have a plural form.

I asked her for some **advice**.
Mix **the water** with **the flour**.

Here are some very common uncountable nouns. Be careful with them, because they may be countable in your own language. Remember that the verb that goes with them must be singular.

advice	furniture	progress
air	happiness	safety
anger	homework	knowledge
beauty	information	money
behaviour	luggage	water
damage	meat	work

The **meat was** not cooked properly.
The **damage has** not been repaired.
The **information** he gave us **was** correct.
Her **behaviour upsets** everyone.

Some/any

You can use **some** and **any** with plural countable nouns and with uncountable nouns.

> I'd like **some potatoes**.
> I haven't got **any shoes**.
> We need to buy **some furniture**.
> Do you have **any milk**?

Many/a few

You can use **many** and **a few** with plural countable nouns but not with uncountable nouns.

> There aren't **many shops** in the village.
> We waited for **a few minutes**.

Much

You can use **much** with uncountable nouns but not with countable nouns.

> You've given me too **much rice**.
> I haven't got **much experience** of working in offices.

A lot of

You can use **a lot of** with plural countable nouns and with uncountable nouns.

> I ate **a lot of biscuits**.
> She suffered **a lot of pain**.

Countable and uncountable

Some nouns can be used in both countable and uncountable ways. Compare the following sentences.

Countable use	Uncountable use
He gave me a box of **chocolates**.	The cake was covered with **chocolate**.
I heard a strange **noise** in the bedroom.	There was too much **noise** to work.
Could you turn on the **light**, please?	Open the curtains to let in some **light**.
He warned them of the **dangers**.	We did not understand the **danger** we were in.

A piece of ...

We use **a piece of ...** with some uncountable nouns to form countable noun phrases.

> She gave me **a** useful **piece of advice**.
> He brought several **pieces of** his own **furniture** with him.
> This is a wonderful **piece of work**.